PRAY

PRAY

A Study of Distinctively Christian Praying

by

CHARLES FRANCIS WHISTON

Professor Emeritus of Systematic Theology
Church Divinity School of the Pacific
Berkeley, California

WILLIAM B. EERDMANS PUBLISHING COMPANY
Grand Rapids, Michigan

To the many faculty members, students, and laymen who have assisted me in the work; to Harold Duling, John Lynn, and Charles Williams of the Lilly Endowment; and in particular to my wife, Jane, who has been my daily companion in prayer.

Contents

Introduction: The Need

Now once he was in a certain place praying, and when he had finished one of his disciples said, "Lord, teach us to pray, just as John taught his disciples." He said to them, "Say this when you pray:

'Father, may your name be held holy,
your kingdom come;
give us each day our daily bread,
and forgive us our sins,
for we ourselves forgive each one who is in debt to us.
And do not put us to the test' " (Luke 11:1-4; Jerusalem
Bible, as throughout).

The need which drew the first disciples of Jesus to him, seeking to learn from him how to pray, is still present in our lives today. We, too, need to be taught how to pray. We need to be taught to pray as Christians, men who belong unashamedly to Jesus Christ. We may be churchmen without prayer, but we cannot be Christians without a life of prayer.

Jesus, the Man of Prayer, commands us to pray. But how shall we obey him if we do not know how to pray and no one can teach us? Too long has it been taken for granted that every Christian, clergy or layman, prays. Both clergy and laity know that the assumption does not hold true in their lives.

When we face the crises of life we realize the poverty, perhaps even bankruptcy, of our life of prayer. At such times we wish we knew much more of prayer than we do. What do we know of prayer really? Selfish petition in time of need; remnants of childish prayers that have no meaning and no power; egocentric, self-seeking prayers—are these truly Christian prayers?

Where could we have learned to pray? From the clergy? What leads us to believe that the clergy know any more about prayer than we do? How many clergy make us believe that they are truly men of prayer? When the clergy prepared us for church baptism, confirmation, or Christian marriage, did they offer us any serious instruction in praying? Did we learn about prayer from any of the Sunday School classes that we attended? Were our teachers there men and women of prayer?

And where, after all, could clergymen have learned to pray? In the theological seminaries which prepared them for the ministry? Were the faculty members under whom they studied truly men of prayer, or only scholars? How many clergy were graduated from seminary as "men of prayer"? One seminary dean told a group of students who had asked help in learning to pray, "You either know how to pray, or you do not, and nothing can be done about it in a seminary."

This book is offered as an invitation from Jesus Christ to sit at his feet and learn from him of the mystery and richness of the life of prayer. It is offered to all people: clergy and laity, young and old, men and women, believers and non-believers, churchmen and nonchurchmen.

It is offered first of all to the laity, the great host of church people, who today feel like sheep without a shepherd. Many laymen are far more hungry to learn and live the authentic life of Christian prayer than the clergy realize. Most "schools of prayer" have arisen at the initiation of the laity. Many laymen are disturbed and disillusioned with the church's attention to everything except the things of God, for they know that without Christ all the myriad activities of the church are worth nothing. They know that without prior obedience to Jesus Christ no service to men will bless the world, and that they must be men of Christ if they are to be servants not *of* the world but *to* the world. This book on distinctively Christian praying is offered to the laity, to lead them to the green pastures of God where they may be fed by the Good Shepherd.

But this book is equally offered to the clergy. So often they are disturbed, bewildered, confused, and frustrated as they are caught up in the maze and tangle of all the schemes and campaigns and techniques of the churches. Were they called by Jesus Christ to be doing all this which seems so fruitless and sterile? Prayerless clergy seeking to serve the praying Christ! Can there be a more vivid antinomy than this?

The clergy know that their laymen expect them to be truly men of prayer, but they know that they are not. When lay people come to them for help in prayer, they have to switch them to something else, perhaps the latest activity of the church. Many are sorely tempted to leave the church. Many more remain in their work with empty, lonely ministries, and sooner or later they break down under the strain. We politely say they are exhausted and give them a vacation, but they return from vacation as empty and jaded as they were before. The real problem is that they are not drinking from the spring of living waters that Christ gives to those who pray. Who has ever taken concern that they should learn to pray? Who cares for them? Have their bishops and superintendents tried to help them become men of prayer? Meetings with bishops and superintendents are too busy with administrative and financial matters to have time for prayer. Did the seminaries that trained them for the ministry give them the ministry of prayer? How many think of their faculty as first of all men of prayer? How many clergy graduated from seminary with any kind of a disciplined life of prayer? The clergy, fully as much as the laity, need to be taught to pray. This book is seriously and humbly offered also to the faculties of the theological seminaries. It is to them that the churches entrust the lives of the young men whom Jesus Christ has called to be his ministers. Jesus Christ calls them as faculty to be not only able scholars but also devout and disciplined examples of praying. How can they help the students to become men of prayer if they themselves do not have an authentic life of disciplined prayer? How many of their students in later years will remember them as men of prayer? Have they prayed for their students and prayed with them?

There are most encouraging signs that seminary faculty members are eager to be men of prayer. Through the "Lilly Endowment Project for the Deepening of the Spiritual Life of the Seminary Faculty" during the past seven years, some fifty faculty men have offered themselves to undergo the disciplines of prayer and to offer teaching to their students in prayer. Out of this there may come a rich harvest of praying clergy and through them a praying laity in the churches.

Moreover, this book is offered to those who scoff at piety, those whose only knowledge of piety is that remaining from childhood days. They have judged prayer by the very little which they knew and discarded it. If they will also read this book, they may find that there are wide horizons of prayer which they have never known and so be encouraged to explore again and more thoroughly the world of prayer. Have they ever seriously studied prayer and truly practiced it, so that their judgments upon it may be trusted? There may be vastly more to prayer than they imagine. There is a great host of praying men and women down through the centuries who have much to teach them, if they will be humble enough to listen. It is hoped that they, too, may read this book and learn to pray.

This book is written, finally, for those people who do pray but whose prayer is almost exclusively petition, either for themselves or for others. They are invited to look steadfastly at the prayer life of Jesus and to learn from him to adventure into vaster, more important dimensions of prayer than they have ever known. Thus their prayer will become more and more like the prayer of Jesus and so more distinctively Christian.

This book has grown out of a study of the place of praying in the curriculum and life of seminaries in the United States and Canada. Sponsored by the Lilly Endowment of Indianapolis, the project began in the spring of 1964 and has continued through the seven years following. John S. Lynn, General Manager of the foundation, had long been concerned about the nearly total absence in American seminaries of serious training either in the study of prayer or in its practice. This concern was shared by Harold Duling, Director for Religion, who early in 1964 attended an interdenominational silent retreat at which I led a group of clergymen into an evaluation of their prayer lives. Soon thereafter Lilly Endowment, Inc. provided a generous grant for the establishment of "A Project for the Deepening of the Spiritual Life of Seminary Students."

I devoted a semester's sabbatical leave to the project, visiting many theological schools and holding retreats for faculty and students. By the end of that time it was clear that the study would require several years to complete, and my seminary in Berkeley very graciously granted me permission to devote part of my time over the next five years to the project. It also became evident that the real target of the project must be, not the students alone, but the faculty. Every three years the student body would change completely and the work would need to be done over again. The real objective, I realized, lay in changing the attitudes and practices of the faculty, who would be the continuing element in the seminaries. The project accordingly became, "The Lilly Endowment Project for the Deepening of the Spiritual Life of the Seminary Faculty." Following the death of Harold Duling, in the spring of 1964, the study received the wholehearted support—both through personal encouragement and through an additional grant—of John Lynn and Charles G. Williams, Mr. Duling's successor as Director for Religion.

In the meantime, my visits to many campuses led students to demand that their faculties help them in learning the life of prayer. "Schools of prayer" were offered to selected groups of faculty men to aid them in this task. Some of the sixty seminaries contacted made no response, but in most of them at least a few faculty members replied and expressed interest. Such schools, offering a few days or several evenings of guidance both in personal prayer and in teaching about it, have been held throughout the country.

In addition, some fifty faculty members in twenty seminaries have become linked together in a "National Trysting Group," supporting one another in seeking the disciplined life of prayer, teaching others concerning prayer, and becoming the spiritual directors of theological students. These men have pledged to meet daily with Jesus Christ in prayer to renew their covenant with him; to intercede regularly for their faculty colleagues and their students; to take time daily for devotional reading of the Bible; and to intercede daily for each member of the National Trysting Group. The group holds an annual weekend conference to pray and worship together and to share with one another their prayer lives and their experiences in teaching courses in prayer. Each man is also writing a spiritual autobiography which will be distributed to all the members, helping them come to know one another spiritually as well as academically. All these efforts, we hope, will ensure that students graduate from seminaries not only with academic knowledge about God but also with the ability to help their parish people become persons of prayer.

Twenty-six seminaries now offer instruction in prayer and help with its practice. But many thousands of lay Christians, as well as students in other seminaries, have no opportunity to receive such personal instruction. This book, therefore, gathers together the most important ideas about prayer which have arisen from discussions and activities with laymen, students, and pastors at many schools and retreats. It is offered as another means to enable all Christians to become men and women of prayer.

Whoever reads this book will soon find that the judgment of Jesus Christ falls on his praying. In what way is our praying different from that of a Jew, Moslem, or Hindu? Should there not be unique marks to Christian praying? Do our prayers use God or offer ourselves to God that he may use us? How many of our prayers are egocentric, seeking our own gain, and how few are devoted to serving God! Are we willing to face the penetrating judgment of Jesus Christ upon our basically pagan praying?

From time to time in our lives, Christ sends us men and women of prayer. We are stirred profoundly as we sense the peace, joy, wisdom, and patience of such lives, and we know intuitively that their quality of life stems from their life with Christ in praying. By comparison we suddenly see the poverty of our own lives of prayer, and we are prompted to take up prayer anew. We begin to pray, but at once we feel bewildered and lost in the world of prayer. We know that we need help but are ashamed to ask for help, and helpers are hard to find. Before we know it our zeal has withered, and our praying becomes intermittent and eventually ceases.

One of the major reasons we give up praying is that we lack any secure foundations for our praying. Prayer that is enduring and stable must be built upon rocklike foundations. This book seeks to offer suggestions for the laying of these foundations.

The life of Christian praying will never be easy. Nothing that is truly important is easy. But that does not mean that it is not possible for every man to have an authentic life of prayer. For the life of prayer comes to us as a gift from Jesus

Christ, not from any efforts to achieve it by ourselves. Christ is more than ready to give us the gift if only we will draw near to him and receive it. All that this book can do is describe the way, to prepare the reader for Christ's coming with the gift.

This book needs to be read in the spirit of prayer, as much with heart and will as with mind. Only as we are led by Christ to practice that which we learn from reading will our reading bless us and make us into men of prayer. Mere study about prayer is not sufficient. It is the practice of prayer that brings ideas to life.

This book will inevitably be a witness to prayer as Jesus Christ has taught me over some forty years. Slowly over these long years the Holy Spirit within me, sent by Christ, has been leading me to Jesus Christ and taking of the life of prayer in him to engraft it into me. It is by no means simply theoretical knowledge about praying which I present. Rather it is the witness of what Jesus Christ has taught me and done with me in prayer to which I bear witness. These insights have been tested, not only in my life, but also in the lives of many others to whom I have been a teacher in prayer. Their experience has confirmed my own. These thoughts on prayer are therefore offered to the reader, not as my gift to him, but as a gift coming from Jesus Christ, using me as his earthen vessel.

Pray as you read. Pray as you reflect. Pray as you decide. Meet the praying Jesus Christ and learn from him. Receive from him the gift of prayer.

Part I

FOUNDATIONS OF PRAYER

Therefore, everyone who listens to these words of mine and acts upon them will be like a sensible man who built his house on rock. Rain came down, floods rose, gales blew and hurled themselves against that house, and it did not fall: it was founded on rock. But everyone who listens to these words of mine and does not act on them will be like a stupid man who built his house on sand. Rain came down, floods rose, gales blew and struck that house, and it fell; and what a fall it had (Matthew 7:24-27).

The life of distinctively Christian praying must be built upon solid foundations. Spasmodic, intermittent, situational praying in times of crisis may be able to rest on the immediate occasion and need. But stable and sustained praying will need to rest on something much more solid and enduring. Praying primarily based upon the felt need of the moment will be a very different kind of praying from that which is rooted and grounded in deep truths concerning both God and man. Prayer may be either egocentric or theocentric, and these are two very different kinds of praying. Let us seek therefore to lay a firm, deep, theological base upon which Christian praying may then be built. Let us begin by turning away from ourselves to Jesus Christ, the man of prayer.

Jesus as Man of Prayer

One indisputable fact that has survived all critical study of the gospels is that the Jesus there presented to us is a man of prayer. So simply, casually, and naturally is Jesus portrayed to us as praying that we may easily overlook this most important factor in his life and ministry. We can simply take it for granted that it is so and pass by without any deeper thought. But it would be utterly unthinkable to picture Jesus Christ without the dimension of prayer. It is perhaps because we read the gospels so often as *unpraying* men that we are insensitive to the deep prayer dimension of his life. For him prayer was not peripheral, casual, or irrelevant but, on the contrary, absolutely central and essential. The first disciples soon recognized something very unusual about his life: his unique wisdom, power and closeness to the invisible God. They surmised rightly that his prayer life held the secret of his unique relation with the Father.

Today, when we are so enamored with the thought of Jesus as the "man for others," we need to look again at the New Testament record, which portrayed him as primarily the "man for God." In his life the first and great commandment to love God above all, really came first. The commandment to love one's neighbor was second in importance and always dependent upon the first commandment. But today our first and greatest concern has become man and man's world. God is relegated at most to second place and often to last place. We tend to be more man-centered and world-centered than God-centered.

Behind all of Jesus' relationships with men lay the even more important relationship with God the Father, whose unique Son he knew himself to be. Thus, when he would teach his disciples to pray, the first concerns to be taken up in praying are the Father's name, the Father's kingdom, and the Father's will. Only after those agenda are finished is there to be concern for the needs of men—for nourishment from God's giving, for forgiveness from the Father so that they may demonstrate the forgiving life to others, and for victory over every evil power.

From Jesus we learn that the first concern in prayer is God, not the benefits that we can get from God for ourselves. God is not a powerful resource to be tapped, exploited, manipulated, and used. He is a person before whom we stand in awe, to whom we bow in glad surrender to be used by him. Our attention to God and his purposes, it is true, will eventually have mighty consequences for men and the world. But both prayer and worship will become distorted and radically misused if they are not rooted first of all in God.

The earliest disciples have reported their deep conviction that Jesus' wisdom, power, serenity, and purity stemmed neither from books nor from human dialogue; rather they issued from his times of being alone in prayer with God. They measured the poverty, weakness, and ignorance of their own lives against his life and realized how much they needed to learn to pray as Jesus did. They sensed that he lived in depths of prayer of which they knew nothing.

The Bible begins with a picture of man, represented by Adam and Eve, living in the immediate presence of God. It is given to us not as scientific history but unmistakably in the form of a myth. Myth and science, of course, are two very different kinds of truth, and we will grossly misunderstand mythical truth if we demand to judge it by the rules of scientific truth. The truth revealed by the Genesis myth is that man's true home is to be with God so that God may dwell with man. In the book of Revelation, closing the Bible, the mythical picture of the final state of man redeemed portrays man as living once again in the immediate presence of God.

> I saw the holy city, and the new Jerusalem, coming down from God out of heaven. . . . Then I heard a loud voice call from the throne, "You see this city? Here God lives among men. He will make his home among them; they shall be his people, and he will be their God" (Revelation 21:2, 3).

The old-Adam life, in separation and independence from God, is a deformation of man's life as it was intended by God in creation. Man's life is not truly human until it is indwelt by God and lived in conscious fellowship with God. In Jesus Christ we see what true human life is. God dwelt in Jesus Christ, and Jesus Christ dwelt with God. We should not consider our life truly human and Jesus' life superhuman. Rather, Jesus' life is the true human life, and ours is sub-human or, even worse, dehumanized.

Our life of praying is a most important index of whether or not we live in God and God in us. To be indwelt by God through Jesus Christ, and to have received the Holy Spirit within us, *must* lead to meaningful prayer. Not to pray is to neglect a most important factor of genuinely human existence. If we read the story of the life of St. Francis of Assisi we find our own lives judged by his deep, Christocentric life. In all of our humanistic studies of man today, the dimension of prayer is seldom mentioned, let alone given adequate treatment. The result is a very distorted picture of what man is. Without prayer, man is not truly man.

In reading through the four gospels let us give special attention to every passage in which Jesus is portrayed to us as the Man of Prayer. Let us keep company with the praying Jesus, watching and listening to him. Then, with his earliest disciples, we will impulsively cry out to him,

Lord, teach us to pray.

Prayer as Relationship

When Jesus prayed, he was not having a monologue with himself or a dialogue with his fellowmen. He was in a real and living objective relationship with the invisible God, whom he addressed as "Father." Although prayer is truly an interior action, yet it is at the same time a truly objective relationship with the invisible, transcendent God.

Our relation with God is radically unlike our relationships with all other things in the created universe. God is not simply one more object, amongst all the other objects in the universe. All created objects exist under the restrictions of time and space, and we know them through our sensory experience of them. But God does not have this kind of corporeality. Although actively immanent, God is at the same time always transcendent over all conditions of space and time.

Let us not be taken in by the popular, shallow, haughty ridicule that God is not "up there" or "out there." Of course, no matter how far into outer space man may venture, he will not there discern an object to be called "God." Nor will any dissection of a human person ever find God there. God is not to be imagined in terms of any created object. If we think we can discover God and use him for our purposes, we are thinking not of God but of an idol. Invisible, intangible, and transcendent as God is, we cannot expect that the modes of perception which we use in relation to all created objects will be adequate to know God. Our relations with creatures will be at best only an analogy of our relation with God. Human language is based upon space-time experiences. In using this earth-bound language to convey to others our experience of

God, we must always remember that our language is an analogy and not at all an accurate description of God. Isaiah recorded a decisive encounter with the living God in the temple at Jerusalem:

> In the year of King Uzziah's death I saw the Lord Jahweh seated on a high throne; his train filled the sanctuary; above him stood seraphs, each one with six wings: two to cover its face, two to cover its feet and two for flying.
>
> And they cried out one to another in this way,
> "Holy, holy, holy is Jahweh Sabaoth.
> His glory fills the whole earth."
>
> The foundations of the threshold shook with the voice of the one who cried out, and the Temple was filled with smoke. I said:
>
> "What a wretched state I am in! I am lost,
> for I am a man of unclean lips
> and I live among a people of unclean lips,
> and my eyes have looked at the King, Jahweh Sabaoth."
>
> Then one of the seraphs flew to me holding in his hand a live coal which he had taken from the altar with a pair of tongs. With this he touched my mouth and said:
>
> "See now, this has touched your lips,
> your sin is taken away,
> your iniquity is purged."
>
> Then I heard the voice of the Lord saying:
>
> "Whom shall I send? Who will be our messenger?"
>
> I answered, "Here I am, send me" (Isaiah 6:1-8).

Even after reading Isaiah's words, we can form no mental image of what God looks like. Only a dim and mysterious imaging of the seraphs is possible. The Holy God remains invisible, formless, hidden. No camera film can record any image, and no tape can record the voice of God. Indeed, if another person had been at Isaiah's side at the very moment of his experiencing God, the other person might not have seen the vision or heard the voice.

Do we mean, then, that it was only a purely subjective, day-dreaming kind of experience that Isaiah had, not caused by any objective act of a transcendent God? The heart of Isaiah's encounter was being confronted by the mysterious presence of the Holy God, of being purged and forgiven, claimed and sent. Crudely to materialize this great spiritual experience of Isaiah is grossly to misunderstand what took place there and then.

Have we in our own life histories any experiences of seeing and hearing God, that may help us understand Isaiah's experience? Can we remember times in our own past when we knew beyond all doubting that we were in the presence of the invisible God? I would share with the reader one such time in my life. With three other men I had spent two weeks camping in the Adirondack Mountains of northern New York State. We camped at Lake Clear Heart in an open-front log cabin on the night of a full moon, the Saturday before Labor Day of 1923. Normally I would have slept soundly till dawn broke. But that night at about two o'clock I found myself suddenly fully awake. I knew I had to get up and dress, and for some hours I walked or sat by the lake, the full moon lighting everything softly. I saw no vision, I heard no voice, but I knew beyond all doubt that an invisible presence which I knew to be God was confronting me. Without words I received the message from God: I was to resign my work with the cotton mills in Boston and offer myself to the church to become a minister of Jesus Christ. There was no emotional excitement. I was as still within as nature was without. I "heard," but did not hear; I "saw," but did not see.

Almost fifty years since then have validated the reality of all that happened to me that night. It was my call from God. I had to obey it, despite numerous obstacles. For anyone who has had such an experience, Isaiah's vision is immediately convincing.

In praying or worshiping we must not seek visual or auditory experiences of God. Although we need to use the language of sight and hearing to articulate our knowledge of God to ourselves and to communicate it to others, we know God through his invisible, inaudible, imageless presence. To look for light waves or sound waves which demonstrate the divine presence is to ask for a sign, and Jesus Christ has expressly warned us that no sign shall be given us on our demand. Our communion with God is by faith, not by sight.

God as Personal

As we pray we need to turn to the highly personalistic, anthropomorphic terminology of the biblical revelation of God. Our culture has a strong tendency to depersonalize and to reduce to abstractions. We have far more success in dealing with things than in dealing with persons. We are able to orbit men in space and land them on the moon, but in social problems involving human, personal relationships we know deep failure. The language we use to describe the working of things cannot fully express relations we have with persons.

It is significant that the incarnation of God in Jesus Christ took place not in Athens but in Palestine, amid a people who unashamedly used anthropomorphic imagery to describe their experiences of the invisible, imageless God. Such person-oriented imagery contrasts sharply with our own thing-oriented language. To which is authentic religious experience more akin? Is God really better described as "it" or as "he"? As "ground of being" (how many people really understand this highly abstract term?) or as "Father"?

The term "Father" is not used in the same sense for God as for our human fathers. And of course to call God "Father" is not to imply that there is also a "Mother," or that God is male.

Every age translates the biblical concept of God into its own philosophical terminology. But through the ages such philosophical substitutions have always proven inadequate, and each age is driven back at last to the biblical terms for an adequate interpretation of its religious experience. We may use philosophical language for *thinking* about God, but when we pray we instinctively return to biblical language.

The life of praying will not be born, let alone grow strong, unless it is nourished upon personalistic conceptions of God. We cannot converse with the impersonal. We do not bow down in awe before the abstract, nor surrender our lives to it. God is surely far more than what we mean by personal in the human sense, and his personhood is beyond the highest human realization of it. Yet images taken from our very limited achievements in personhood are a better likeness to God than those taken from our relationships with the world of things.

Our experience of prayer as speaking with God and his speaking with us must be couched in personal terms. We are not to apologize nor be ashamed for this but to glory in it. Jesus Christ himself gave us the precious privilege of addressing God as "Father." We do not need the permission of any theologian or philosopher to validate our using that name for God. To abandon the biblical terminology for God in favor of philosophical and psychological terminology, abstract and impersonal as they are, does not throw light upon the issue but beclouds it.

We all have deep, perhaps subconscious reasons for preferring an impersonal God to a personal one. Our relation to the impersonal is aimed at control and domination for our profit. We do not feel guilt before the abstract and impersonal. We may err, but we do not sin. Before a personal God, however, we know that we ever face moral and spiritual judgment, conviction of sin, and his claim to own and use us for his purposes.

When we pray we draw near to God as personal. Otherwise we shall not pray at all, or prayer will be only talking to ourselves. C. S. Lewis spoke to this issue in *The Problem of Pain:*

> . . . I find it easier to believe in a myth of gods and demons than in one of the hypostatized abstract nouns. And after all, our mythology may be much nearer the literal truth than we suppose (p. 123).

The Prevenience of God

We are prone to look upon all human experience from an egocentric perspective. The "I" is the starting point from which all of our experience begins. We like to believe that every verb has "I" for its subject. So habituated are we to this perspective that we take it for granted as a basic axiom of all life, including our praying. I pray and thereby seek to get God's attention and his gifts.

Religious experience in the Bible has a very different starting point. The great agent in the Bible record is God, not man. God is subject; man is object. The biblical history tells of God's seeking, finding, choosing, claiming, judging, forgiving, training, correcting, and using man for his purposes. The Scriptures say nothing of a hit-or-miss human search after God. Abraham, Moses, the prophets, John the Baptist, Paul, and, supremely, Jesus were all religious leaders raised up by God, not volunteers whom God accepted.

Because of our chronic egocentricity we think of ourselves as initiating prayer. We seek after God to gain his attention, to have him come into our presence, to respond to our desires and do our will. We will pray far better if we reverse the roles and think of God as seeking to hold our attention, reveal his will to us, and evoke our response. In the most ancient liturgies of the church the Lord's Prayer was customarily introduced by a reminder that we pray it because Jesus Christ has taught us and commanded us so to pray:

> As our Saviour Christ hath commanded us and taught us, we are bold to say: "Our Father . . . " (*The Book of Common Worship of the Church of South India*, p. 17).

Every impulse and desire to pray, every act of prayer, has

behind it the mysterious, hidden, and easily overlooked motivation of the Holy Spirit within us, calling us and moving us to pray. How very different are the words that Job spoke to God after God bade him keep silent and listen, from those he presumed to address to God on his own initiative.

Very seldom does a person initiate a thought process, a memory, or a mental image. It would be more accurate for us to say, "The thought just now came to me," than to say, "I think." We are made to remember, often against our will and inclination. Our memory is touched and set into motion by the action of another, mysteriously hidden within us. Not all thoughts come from the Holy God. But as each thought comes, we can give it our attention and examine it in the light of the presence of the invisible Jesus Christ. Thus we may sort out these inner thoughts, desires, memories, and imaginations. Some of them we know instantly do not belong to Christ or come from him, and these we let drop and turn away from. To those that seem in harmony with Christ's presence we give our attention, seeing where they take us. It is in this way that God speaks to us within.

So dulled are we to the divine prevenience that we sorely need to pause a moment before every act of prayer and let ourselves be reminded that we are about to pray because God himself is seeking us in prayer, calling us to enter into this relation with him. Thus all praying is an act of obedient response to God. Christ calls us; we come. He commands us; we obey. This is especially true of regular, habitual praying. We do such praying not because we feel like it but because God is calling us to keep the tryst of prayer with him. He is already there waiting for us to come. St. Benedict of Nursia emphasized to his monks that, when they rose from bed to pray together nightly in the chapel or oratory, they could never precede God. God was always there waiting, expecting them.

Realization of God's prevenience will keep us from feverish, anxious, frustrating efforts to realize the presence of God in ways of our choosing. He is already there before we even begin to pray. We are in his presence, and he seeks to give us the gift of being present to us. Robert Frost has this wisdom to give to us:

> I turned to speak to God
> About the world's despair;
> But to make bad matters worse
> I found God wasn't there.
> God turned to speak to me
> (Don't anybody laugh)
> God found I wasn't there—
> At least not over half.
> (*The Poems of Robert Frost,* pp. 357-358)

Why is it that very few textbooks of theology contain any reference to the action of God as prevenient? True, the theological term is not a biblical one, but the Bible is filled with the fact of divine prevenience. In the pericope of the burning bush, it was not Moses who was seeking Jahweh. Rather it was Jahweh seeking, calling, and claiming Moses. Jeremiah bore witness to the prevenience of God in calling him even before his birth to be a prophet to the nations. All through his ministry Jesus waited for the green light of God's appointed time as the sign for his action.

In all of our praying we need to begin with the recollection that God is again calling us to come. Our role is not that of initiating prayer but of obedient response. We speak to God in prayer because he has first spoken to us, just as we love God because, as John observed, God first loved us. All prayer is an act of obedience. Not to respond to God's invitation is to sin against him.

We tend not to recognize the prevenient action of God toward us and upon us, for we do not want to root our praying in obedience. We prefer to ground our prayer in our own need and desire, praying when we want to or need to. The realization that true prayer is always an obedient response is one of the deepest lessons in prayer that we need to learn—and continually relearn if our praying is to become habitual and regular.

Remember the Lord's explicit command to the three disciples in Gethsemane, "Keep awake and pray." They disobeyed, and when the powers of evil came upon them they were utterly unprepared. Jesus obeyed the invitation of his Father. He kept awake and prayed, and when the hour came, his praying gave him the strength to be victorious.

Prayer and Grace

Prayer will ever run the danger of being rooted in self-effort and self-will rather than in dependence upon God and his will. If we think that prayer is what we do on our own initiative, then prayer becomes a form of righteousness by works: because we pray, we may soon conclude, God must reward us as we desire.

Of course prayer does have rewards, but rewards must not be our motivation for praying. Rewards come as gifts. It will never be easy to keep prayer free from the deadly sin of pride. We remember the vivid parable of Jesus:

> Two men went up to the Temple to pray, one a Pharisee, the other a tax collector. The Pharisee stood there and said this prayer to *himself,* "*I* thank you, God, that *I* am not grasping, unjust, adulterous, like the rest of mankind, and particularly that *I* am not like this tax collector here. *I* fast twice a week; *I* pay tithes on all *I* get." The tax collector stood some distance away, not daring even to raise his eyes to heaven; but he beat his breast and said, "God, be merciful to me, a sinner." This man, I tell you, went home again at rights with God; the other did not (Luke 18:10-14, italics mine).

Prayer is as much the gift of God as is forgiveness. Only if we are constantly aware that we pray by grace, not by self-will, shall we avoid the danger of sinful praying. When we obey in the disciplines of prayer our first thought will be, "Well, we have done it." But deeper thinking will lead us to attribute our obedience to God, not to self-mastery. We shall impulsively and thankfully cry out,

> *Thanks be to thee, O God, that by thy grace I have been enabled to keep these disciplines of prayer.*

We shall *begin* our life of prayer depending very largely, if not exclusively, upon our own will and effort. We shall grit our teeth and make ourselves to pray, especially if we decide to follow a set of rules for praying. Then we find ourselves right back in the old pattern of religious effort, seeking to keep the law and thus earn merit with God. We need constantly to be reminded that we live not by a set of rules, however good those rules may be, but in the presence of a person, Jesus Christ. Our obedience is personal obedience to him, not obedience to an impersonal set of rules. I pray not because I must keep a set of rules but because Jesus Christ calls me into a tryst with him, rooted in thankfulness for his gracious dealing with me in the past:

> *Because thou hast dealt so graciously with me, therefore I come to thee to pray.*

It is one thing to break impersonal rules: how little we hesitate to break traffic laws. It is quite another matter not to keep the tryst with Jesus Christ and thus to grieve and disappoint him. No set of rules, but only the person Christ, can call us into prayer.

Prayer which is rooted in self-will and self-determination will be strained, exhausting, and frustrating. Prayer under grace, on the other hand, will gradually become almost effortless, as natural as breathing, and full of the wondrous peace that comes from loving obedience to the Lord Jesus Christ.

Christocentric Praying

Throughout the New Testament runs the theme that our access as sinners to God the Father is through Jesus Christ, his obedient Son. In our praying we are accustomed to give lip service to this important fact, by ending our prayers with, "through Jesus Christ our Lord," or, "in Jesus' name we pray." But do we really believe that our *only* access to the Holy God is through him? Have we not allowed humanism to convince us that each of us has direct, unmediated access to God apart from Jesus Christ?

In these days when demythologizing is so prevalent, we tend to pay little attention to the ancient biblical myths. But in the Genesis stories, given to us in the form of myths, we are confronted with very important and abiding religious axioms which we cannot afford to scorn. The Genesis stories were written at a time of high culture and mature religious life. The unknown authors knew just as well as we sophisticated moderns do that serpents do not speak a human language and that God has ever been invisible to human perceptions. These ancient writers were not attempting to write scientific anthropology but were giving us in story form simple, vivid, unforgettable truths concerning the existing relations between God and man. Men, represented by Adam and Eve, were intended to live in immediate communion with God in the Garden of Eden. They were to see and hear God in direct encounter. But when the ground rules of the Garden were broken, then there were immediate and lasting consequences: banishment from the Garden and from immediate access to God's presence, and the beginning of the power of death. Now there existed an uncrossable gulf between disobedient man and the Holy God. Angels with flaming swords guarded all approaches to God. God takes himself and his holiness very seriously, even though man does not.

One of the deepest religious convictions of the saints of God is that of their unworthiness to stand before the Holy God. Shallow, egocentric religion will not be sensitive to the holiness of God. Mature, authentic religious faith will. A prayer in the liturgy of the Church of South India reminds us of this fact:

> *Holy Father, who through the blood of thy dear Son hast consecrated for us a new and living way to thy throne of grace, we come to thee through him, unworthy as we are . . .(The Book of Common Worship, p. 14).*

God has been teaching through the centuries that by nothing man can do from his side of the gulf may he win access to God—not by good works, not by correct thinking, not by sacrifices, and not by sinful, egocentric praying and worshiping. God himself has set up a place where he will draw near to sinful man: the trysting place of the cross of Jesus Christ. There the Holy God will accept sinful man, and man will not be burnt up in the consuming fire of holiness.

The terrible words of Jesus from his cross are the classic exposition of this basic religious truth. After some six hours of silence on the cross there came from Jesus' lips those amazing, unforgettable words, "My God, my God, why hast thou forsaken me?"

We may not dispose of those words by believing that Jesus was mistaken, that he was not really forsaken by God but was psychologically deluded. Nor is he really quoting the entire Twenty-second Psalm—when we quote a few words or a clause from a Psalm, are we quoting the entire Psalm? Have we even any partial comprehension of the experience through which Jesus was going? The words recorded by both Mark and Matthew have the ring of stark objectivity to them.

Paul wrote, "For our sake God made the sinless one into

sin . . . " (2 Corinthians 5:21). When confronted with sinful
man, the Holy God does two things. He withdraws his
presence, and he turns over the sinner to the destroying
power of death. When Jesus stood there as the representative
of the whole sinful human race, the cross became the place of
sin and the tree of cursing. The Holy God cannot and will not
accept sin. He withdrew his presence from Jesus and let the
power of death have dominion over him. Our Lord appar-
ently did not expect this withdrawal of the Father's presence,
and he cried out, "Why?" No answer came.

Our humanist age is determined not to accept the biblical
revelation of the holy wrath of God against evil. We are so
accustomed to tolerate evil and make terms with it that we
are permissive of everything. We insist that God shall be like
us, tolerant and permissive of all things. We live in the
kingdom of evil. We cannot even imagine, so dulled are our
consciences, life where no sin is tolerated. The Bible's delin-
eation of man is radically different from the humanist's. How
very seldom does our age use the word "sin." Where there is
no sense of sin there will be no sense of God's wrath.

In the Passion story there are two important cups. One is
in the upstretched hands of Jesus in the Upper Room, and by
his use of the wine in that cup Jesus is offering his own
lifeblood to the Father as a sacrifice for sin. The second cup
is in the hands of the Father, stretched down to the praying
Jesus in the Garden of Gethsemane. The obedient Son is
commanded to drink it to the dregs. Again and again in the
Old Testament Jahweh had commanded rebellious, faithless
Israel to drink of the cup of his wrath. Here in the Garden it
is Jesus, the obedient one in whom the Father is well pleased,
who is to drink vicariously the cup of the wrath of God. Sin
must meet the judgment of God. Here Jesus stands in the
place of sin, the representative of every sinful man in the
human race for all times.

A new covenant is now wrought by God through Jesus on

the cross. No longer is man to go to a temple at Jerusalem, or to any other temple, to meet the invisible Holy God. The new place of meeting is not a temple or an altar but a towering cross, with the figure upon it of the risen Jesus Christ as King of Kings and Lord of Lords. We sinners must go there, and there the Holy God will welcome and receive us, judge us, forgive us, re-create us, and save us.

This basic truth, that our access to the Holy God is always mediated for us by Jesus Christ, will have great import for our praying. In every act of prayer, in obedience to the mysterious and hidden action of the indwelling Holy Spirit, we shall begin by going into the presence of Jesus Christ. It is in praying to him that we pray to the transcendent Father. We go first of all to the interceding Christ, and then with him intercede to the Father. We have not truly realized the chronic, deep-seated sinfulness that characterizes our life until we know that by ourselves we are shut out from God the Father and that our only access to him is through Jesus Christ. We might well begin every act of prayer with this initial prayer to Jesus Christ:

> *O Lord Jesus Christ, in obedience to thy call and by thy grace, I come to thee, that in thee I may meet the Father and with thee pray to him.*

A former Jewish man, now a minister of Christ, shared with me the account of his conversion to Jesus Christ. In Nazi Germany, as a young boy, he had witnessed the torture and death of parents and grandparents. He had been taken by the underground to Holland, there to live in the home of a deeply Christian family. As a Jew he knew of the holiness of God. He knew also at first hand the terrible sinfulness of man, from his life in Nazi Germany. He knew intuitively that holiness and sinfulness cannot be together. A mediator was needed to cross that deep gulf of separation. That mediator he found in the Christian witness of the family with whom he lived for the war years. Only by mediation did he dare to come into the presence of the Holy God.

Humanism today has departed sharply from the apostolic evaluation of the person and work of Jesus Christ. A very important issue is at stake here, with tremendous consequences for our praying. Who is Jesus Christ for *us?* Is he but a blueprint or pattern? Is he simply an outstanding example of that which is really latent in us all? Does he represent the inherent divinity in every man? Is he the revelation of man, not of God? If we look to him as example and pattern there is no real reason why we should not achieve his stature and even surpass it.

Humanism proclaims the dignity and greatness of man. See what man has accomplished in our own lifetime! But over against man's very real and great accomplishments there stands the dire record of his inhumanity to man and his careless despoliation of nature. The dignity and worth of man in the Bible is offered to man by God though his work in Jesus Christ. Man's value is rooted in obedience to God and dependence on him.

Christocentric prayer demands a very high view of Christ. C. S. Lewis has attested that the Christ of humanism would never have won him from paganism. There is a deep concomitance between Christology and prayer. In this respect perhaps our hymns, strongly emphasizing the importance of Christ, are a wiser guide to follow than are many of our contemporary theological writings, so dominated by skepticism and doubt.

The Creator-Creature Relationship

The Holy Scriptures begin by setting before us our stature as creatures over against the Creator God. All other objects with which we have relationships share with us this creatureliness. God, however, is not another creaturely object but Creator and Sustainer. Before any created beings had existence, he existed eternally. All other objects have their beginning in time, exist for a time, and then die. But this is not true of God. He eternally is, even though such existence is forever beyond our experience or comprehension. Our existence is a derived and dependent existence. We owe our being to him.

"It is he who hath made us,/And not we ourselves." We receive our existence as a holy gift from God, and we perpetually depend upon him for continuance. We are neither self-originated nor self-sustained.

God's existence is radically different from ours. His existence had no beginning in time. In no way is his existence or continuance dependent upon us. He has life and being in himself, *a se* as the theologians term it. We need God for our existence; God does not need us for his.

We can never escape, here or hereafter, from this status of creaturehood. Yet deep in all of us is the ineradicable desire to be on our own, to be independent from God, to belong to ourselves. We want God to be a means to our own ends, and our prayers are often attempts to use God as an omnipotent resource to be tapped to serve our desires.

We were created for dependent, obedient existence, for theocentric rather than egocentric life, ever receiving from God all that he gives to us. In our praying we must never lose sight of this vast difference between God the Creator and

Sustainer and ourselves as creatures. We do not enter into the dialogue of prayer as equals in status. Forever it will remain a mighty miracle that God bestows upon his creature man the gift of personal communion and fellowship. The vast and exalted God reaching toward the little creature Man—what paradox could be greater than this? Our prayer must ever contain the note of awe and wonder that such communion is possible.

> *Jahweh, our Lord,*
> *how great your name throughout the earth!*
>
> *I look up at your heavens, made by your fingers,*
> *at the moon and stars you set in place—*
> *ah, what is man that you should spare thought for him,*
> *the son of man that you should care for him?* (Psalm 8:1, 3-4)

God-Transcendent and Immanent

In all of our praying we shall need to keep in proper balance the transcendence and immanence of God. Authentic religious experience always bears witness to both of these aspects of our relationship to God. Often we tend to exaggerate one side of the paradox, ignoring the other. In contemporary religious thinking we are almost exclusively concerned for "God in man," and we are neglecting the biblical fact of God's transcendence.

We need to acknowledge unashamedly that God does not fit neatly into the categories of man's thinking and experiences. Man is never the measure of God. God does not and will not meet our human specifications of what we think God must be but always confronts us in baffling mystery. The more we are given to know him, the deeper becomes the mystery of God. Let us hearken humbly to this ancient wisdom:

> We could say much more and still fall short;
>   to put it concisely, "He is all."
> Where shall we find sufficient power to
>   glorify him,
>   since he is the Great One, above all his
>   works,
> the awe-inspiring Lord, stupendously great,
>   and wonderful in his power?
> Exalt the Lord in your praises
>   as high as you may—still he surpasses you.
> Exert all your strength when you exalt him,
>   do not grow tired—you will never come
>   to the end.
> Who has ever seen him to give a description?

Who can glorify him as he deserves?
Many mysteries remain even greater than these,
   for we have seen only a few of his works,
The Lord himself having made all things—
   and having given wisdom to devout men.
                              (Ecclesiasticus 43:27-33)

Let us not be at all ashamed to use the biblical terminology of "up" and "down," of "heaven" and "earth." The
biblical writers were not using scientific language but the
language of poetry. Love does not use scientific language to
express itself. Our earthly language has to resort to space-
time images derived from our perceptual experience, and
from these we make our abstractions. The word "up" has
more than its spatial meaning. When I say, "I look up to that
person," I surely do not mean that I have to tilt my head to
look at him because he is taller than I. I mean rather that I
respect and honor him as morally and spiritually "above" me.
I can use a spatial word to say this.

In our praying we need constantly to realize that we do
not stand in a relation of equality with God. He forever
"towers above us." It amazes us that the high and exalted
God should "stoop" to having a loving personal relationship
with us. People impulsively knelt before Jesus, for they knew
that he lived far "above" them and their posture of kneeling
expressed that. John the Baptist said a similar thing when he
cried out, "I am not fit to kneel down and undo the strap of
his sandals" (Mark 1:7b).

We look up at God, never down. Why is it that in the
religious architecture of all faiths the altar or sanctuary is
elevated from the rest of the church or temple? Why did the
ancient Greeks build their acropoli on hill tops? In the
theater we look down upon the stage and the action of the
performers. In the house of God our eye instinctively looks
up.

God ever remains hidden and mysterious to us, which we symbolize in terms of distance and unapproachable light. It is not that as we become spiritually mature the mystery of God will disappear. We shall always apprehend far more than our intellects can comprehend. There is so much in God's nature that cannot ever be expressed in human terms. The revelation of God in Jesus Christ does not at all mean that the mystery of God is spelled out so clearly that there is no mystery left. All through the Bible the theophanies of God are accompanied by deep mystery, hiddenness, or dazzling light in which nothing can be discerned. Clouds, deep darkness, blinding light—these always accompany the presence of God.

Paradoxically, authentic religious experience always bears witness to the equally mysterious immanence of God. God dwells hidden in his creature man. The term "Holy Spirit" stands for this deep, abiding indwelling of God in us. The God who is so exalted in the highest heavens also makes us the temples in which he dwells and meets us. God speaks to us and acts in us, not only from without but from within. One of the continual cries of worshiping and praying man is this,

Take not thy Holy Spirit from me.

In true praying and worshiping we know beyond all doubt our utter unworthiness to be the temples in which the Holy God dwells. But were he to withdraw his presence from us, we would perish. We know paradoxically that we are not worthy of his indwelling and also, by his grace, that he will never desert us.

We must be forever attentive to God's speaking to us, both from outside us and from within us.

I am listening. What is Jahweh saying? (Psalm 85:8)

Too much of our praying is talking *at* God, monologue instead of dialogue. Praying must involve listening to God.

Job had to learn that lesson thoroughly before he received the gift of peace from God.

Christian praying, giving due attention to the work of the Holy Spirit within us, brought to us by Jesus Christ from the Father, will learn gradually that many of the thoughts within us arise from the Holy Spirit and not the self. Every impulse to pray, and even the words of prayer, will be seen to be given by the indwelling of God, the Holy Spirit.

The Agape God

"God is love" seems such a truism that we take it for granted. It is the very nature of God to love us. In the New Testament, however, it is never taken for granted but is always an amazing miracle. Paul never ceased to marvel that Christ Jesus, whom he had so violently persecuted in the persons of his followers, had confronted him, claimed him, forgiven him, and given him the gift of *agape*, with all its re-creating power to make him into a new person in Christ.

In our contemporary language love has become terribly debased and degraded, as we see in current moving pictures and literature. It is characterized by egocentricity, seeking one's own satisfaction, and using another person as a thing. It is far more concerned with self-gratification than with the fulfilment of the other. True, our age has seen the breaking of many unhealthy Puritanical standards of sex, yet it is difficult to believe that the license of today is a satisfying answer.

The Greek language is much more precise in this regard than is our English language. Plato, writing of his great master Socrates, dealt at length with *eros*, distinguishing between vulgar and high *eros*. *Eros* love is rooted in an inner need. Man is incomplete and unfulfilled, left to himself. He must turn out from himself to seek those objects which will fulfill his incomplete life. He first of all turns to things, believing that possession of things will bring peace and satisfaction.

Many persons today start out believing that if they can only acquire and possess money and the things that money can buy, then they will be happy. Slowly and deeply God teaches man that his life does not consist in the abundance of things which he possesses. If possessions could bring happiness, then we Americans with our huge supply of gadgets should be the happiest of all peoples, and we are not. "The deceitfulness of riches" is an undebatable axiom of all human life, even though each generation has to learn it anew. When we have decisively learned that possession of things does not satisfy us, then we believe that we shall find satisfaction in persons. Friendships, love, marriage and family—these will fulfill us. But the discouraging evidence of life is that even these at their best and highest still leave within us an emptiness.

No creature, thing, or person can ever slake the thirst placed in us by God the Creator. He has created us for himself, not for the world or for self. This going out from the self, seeking to find, own, possess, and use objects for our fulfilment is certainly part of God's purpose for us. But this *eros*-motivated search is not an end but a preparation for the invasion into our lives of the invisible and Holy God, giving us his own *agape* love. We do not find but are found. We do not search and find; we are entered and filled with God's love.

Eros love always involves a note of ownership, possession, and use. How much parental love is possessive, and how very often married love and friendships are possessive! Our language betrays this fact, for we so often use the possessive pronoun "my" in speaking of wife or husband, child or friend. *Eros* love does not dare to give full freedom. It fears to lose the beloved. It is significant that the Greek word *eros* is not to be found in any of the New Testament writings. In the post-apostolic writings it often appears, but not once in the New Testament. The biblical writers had great discernment in this matter. They knew that the love that had entered their lives from God through Jesus Christ was not *eros* but love of a very different kind. To give expression to this distinctive kind of love they made use of a Greek word seldom used: *agape*.

In Paul's letter to the Christians at Corinth he has written
for us a great hymn to *agape*:

> *Agape* is always patient and kind; it is never jealous; *agape* is
> never boastful or conceited; it is never rude or selfish; it does not
> take offense, and is not resentful. *Agape* takes no pleasure in
> other people's sins but delights in the truth; it is always ready to
> excuse, to trust, to hope, and to endure whatever comes.
>
> *Agape* does not come to an end. But if there are gifts of
> prophecy, the time will come when they must fail; or the gift of
> languages, it will not continue for ever; and knowledge—for this,
> too, the time will come when it must fail (I Corinthians 13:4-8,
> with the word *"agape"* replacing the word "love").

When we measure our love with Paul's picture of the *agape* of
Jesus Christ, all of us know that we are judged as failures.
Our loves and our friendships so often wither and die. Our
loves are full of jealousy and selfishness.

Agape stands for the outpoured, self-giving love from God
to sinful man. It is not given because a man is worthy—what
man could ever dare to claim that he is worthy of the love of
God in Christ? It is offered to us even when God foreknows
that we shall refuse or misuse it. So did Jesus offer *agape* love
to the traitor Judas in the Garden. It is given with full
foreknowledge that it will involve deep and lasting suffering to
God, the giver. It is a love that seeks not its own; it seeks
to give, not to get. The Franciscans called it "love without
desire." It is a love which bestows true freedom and is fully
prepared to meet with every misuse of that freedom. It is a
love which inevitably includes judgment—piercing judgment
upon our egocentric, selfish living. It is a love which accepts
us just as we are but will not leave us as we are. It is a love
which is forgiving and re-creating. In no way is it a permissive,
tolerant love. We dare not speak of the *agape* God unless at
the same time we remember that the *agape* of God is the

agape of a Holy God. So much love today is without judgment, wholly permissive, and utterly unable to redeem and
re-create the person; *agape* love is not at all of this kind.

The New Testament also presents us with the command to
love our neighbor, carrying *agape* to our fellowman. We speak
much today of "loving oneself," of "accepting oneself."
Perhaps we have been misled by the Jewish commandment of
love, based on Deuteronomy 6:4-5 and Leviticus 19:18:

> Listen, Israel: Jahweh our God is the one Jahweh. You shall
> love Jahweh your God with all your heart, with all your soul,
> with all your strength.
>
> You must love your neighbor as yourself.

In Mark 12:29 it is Jesus himself who gives this summary of
the law. In Luke 10:25-28 a lawyer repeats it. Sunday after
Sunday in the liturgies of the churches we hear this ancient
summary of the law. But what is there distinctively Christian
in it? We do have the Christian variation on that theme in
John: "This is my commandment: love one another, as I have
loved you" (John 15:12). We would do well to rephrase the
summary of the law to read, "You must love your neighbor
as I have loved you."

Distinctively Christian love toward man is *agape,* not *eros.*
God desires that we shall become the carriers of *agape* to our
fellowman. God would thus give us the joy of sharing in his
love for man. As we meet the *agape* God in our praying we
shall find ourselves naturally loving with *agape*—loving the
loveless and loving our enemies. We shall know more and
more that the origin of the *agape* we show is not the self but
Christ.

In addition to love for things and persons, there is the
dimension of love toward God. *Eros* love for God is common
and is found in all religious faiths. But distinctively Christian
love for God involves thankfulness and obedience, not simply

eros. John made very clear the note of obedience in Christian love for God:

> As the Father has loved me,
> so I have loved you.
> Remain in my love (John 15:9).
>
> If you keep my commandments
> you will remain in my love,
> just as I have kept my Father's
>   commandments
> and remain in his love (John 15:10).
>
> Anybody who receives my commandments
>   and keeps them
> will be one who loves me (John 14:21).

Paul's dominant expression for love to God is eucharist, which means "thanksgiving." We love God because we have been the recipients of God's *agape.* As we grow in Christian praying we shall find that prayers of thankfulness abound and become as natural as breathing.

Fellowship in Praying

At first sight it seems that we are alone when we pray; but second sight will reveal to us that this is not so. It is more than thinking about God or speaking prayer words to ourselves. Always we pray with the Holy Spirit, who dwells in us. So mysteriously is he hidden within is that we find difficulty in distinguishing between his action and ours. Ultimately, as we live in the Spirit and he in us, he not only impels us to pray but also gives us the very words of our prayers. He prays in us, with us, and for us.

But fellowship in prayer takes us into another relationship also. When we pray, we do not pray alone but join in a great worldwide fellowship extending through the centuries. While we pray, thousands of others are also engaged in prayer to God. We do not see them and are not aware of them, but God sees them. When Elijah complained that he was the only one in all Israel left faithful to God, God immediately corrected his very faulty arithmetic. There were some seven thousand others, unknown to Elijah, who had not bowed the knee to Baal (1 Kings 19:9-18). In praying we enter not only into fellowship with those now living upon this earth, but also into the vastly greater fellowship of all the praying men and women of past ages, from the time of Abraham down to our own day. We keep company with all the praying saints of God—Paul, Francis of Assisi, Brother Lawrence, Fénelon, Francis de Sales, Vincent de Paul, Abbé Huvelin of Paris, all who have called upon the name of God.

We need constantly to be reminded of this vast dimension of prayer, for we easily forget it just because of its invisibility. Whenever I say the Anglican Daily Offices alone, I always begin with this initial prayer:

O Lord Jesus Christ, in obedience to thy call, I come to thee, to join in with thy holy church through all the ages, to acknowledge thee to be the Lord, to pray with them and with thee.

Thus I consciously join in a great chorus of prayer that is constantly going on. I am never really alone but am surrounded by a great company of praying people—an invisible host.

Prayer and Authority

When we pray we seek to enter into a relationship with the power who rightly has totalitarian authority over our lives. God commands; he asks us to obey. Today we are witnessing a widespread revolt against all human authorities—family, nation, church, society—because they have been found to be manifestly inadequate and undeserving authorities. We cannot and will not obey those whom we do not fully respect. Yet we were created to obey God, and our hearts will know nothing but restlessness until we are found by God and surrender our lives to obey and serve him. In prayer that is habitual and disciplined, we regularly present ourselves to him who alone has the right to command and use us. We find deep and abiding peace in the surrender of ourselves to him as our King.

God is our King, not our president. Our passion for democracy may make us reluctant subjects of this King. In democracy the ultimate authority rests in the hands of the people, and we carefully provide a system of checks and balances to limit the power and authority of our elected representatives. But in praying we are face to face with one who is truly our King, not at all subject to our demands. He is not accountable to us, but we to him. We have no voice in his kingship. He is King not by our suffrage but by the Father's appointment. Our role is not to advise and consent but to surrender, serve, and obey.

Deep within all of us is a chronic resistance to such unconditioned belonging to God. We want to benefit from God while retaining our self-sovereignty. Thus all praying involves a mighty siege against the sovereign selfhood by the kingly Christ, offering us the holy gift of joy and peace which come to us when we live under Christ as King. Until each man has been found by Christ and has accepted him as King, he will know only misery, fear, boredom, frustration.

We were made for and are ever called into the life of obedience, which the obedient Son of God alone can give to us. This note of authority and obedience, we shall see, plays a most important role in our life of prayer, as we seek to understand and to practice the kind of prayer which involves surrender to God's claim upon us in Jesus Christ.

God-Means or End?

Men are prone to approach God to use him for their own advantage. Hardly do we appear in God's presence but we quickly take out our shopping lists and inform him what we want and need. We are more concerned to use him as a means to our ends than to offer ourselves to him for his purposes. We are more familiar with *eros* than with *agape*. Prayer that is praise and adoration is much less familiar to us than is petition, despite the New Testament counsel that "it is more blessed to give than to receive."

Does God exist for us, or do we exist for him? Does God exist for our benefit and profit, or do we exist for his glory? In our human relationships we resent it when others use us as means to their ends, preferring the company of those who come not to use us but to enjoy just being with us. If we suspect that someone has come to use us for his gain, we are at once on our guard. What a difference there is between a child's saying to his returning father, "Dad, what have you got for me?" and saying, "O Dad, how glad I am to see you."

An essential part of truly Christian praying is that of praise and adoration, in which we honor God as our end and do not use him as our means.

Spontaneity and Regularity

Shall we pray only when we feel like praying? Shall our praying be left to the whim of inclination? Many people fear that regular, habitual praying is mechanical, worthless, and even sinful.

Prayer is giving our attention to God. But ought our attending to God to be left to those few moments of life when we feel like giving God our attention? Do we love God so truly and deeply that we can leave our praying to fickle feeling? Or is God not far more often seeking to gain our attention than we are prone to give it?

Life must include both spontaneity and regularity. Consider our eating habits. Children would gladly eat whenever they felt like it. But if allowed to do so, they would not eat their regular meals or would eat the wrong things. Three times daily, quite apart from feeling hungry, whether in the mood to eat or not, we stop what we are doing and sit down to eat. Only so will our bodies be rightly nourished. Yet the regularity of these three meals does not preclude times of spontaneity. A friend may drop in, and we may have a cup of tea or coffee with him. Or if we go out to a concert and return home late at night, a little snack is in order.

We teach our children the habit of cleaning their teeth regularly. We do not leave this task at the mercy of inclination or mood. As a result, teeth are kept clean. Habit ensures that teeth will be cleaned, quite apart from mood.

Prayer is intended as much to *im*press on us the need for right relations with God as to *ex*press what we actually feel. Baron von Hügel told of kissing his daughter to awaken his love for her, not only to express his love for her.

God deserves that his creatures come into his presence to

pray and worship regularly. Without the aid of habit, both our prayer and our worship will be irregular and spasmodic. There was great wisdom in the Jewish practice of keeping the Sabbath and the great feasts in the temple at Jerusalem. Their attendance was not left to chance but was required, in obedience to commands. In the New Testament we find a firm but loving rebuke to those who have given up attendance at the Sunday worship: "Do not stay away from the meetings of the community, as some do" (Hebrews 10:25).

We prefer to ask psychological questions rather than theological ones. In our egotism we ask, "Do I want to pray?" "Do I feel like praying?" Often the honest reply to those questions is, "No, I do not." And we do not pray. But if instead we ask the theological question, "Does Christ want me to come to him and pray?" it is difficult to believe that the answer is "No." Prayer and worship are duties to God, not favors we offer him.

Today we are all far more concerned with getting our rights than with performing our duties. All too often we ignore God's rights from us, and our lax, casual church attendance and praying will have dire results. The title of this book is the imperative form of the word "Pray." Prayer is not something we may do or not do as we choose. It is an essential duty of man to God. Habit and regularity will ever be needed by us to assure that we do not neglect God. We need to be reminded to come to God whenever it is "the hour of prayer."

Far from hampering or crowding out spontaneous praying, habit will make us all the more likely to pray on a moment's impulse. We shall have our intercessory lists for habitual times of prayer, but we shall also find ourselves interceding as events happen to us in the course of the day.

As we now turn to considering some of the more important facets of praying, let us always keep in mind these theological truths concerning God and man, so that our praying will rest upon solid, rock-like foundations.

Part II
FACETS OF PRAYING

The life of prayer may be compared to a multifaceted precious stone. Each facet belongs to the totality of the stone and enhances the beauty of every other facet, but no single facet is the whole stone. So prayer consists of many facets of relationship with God, and each facet of prayer needs to be supplemented by the other facets if prayer is to be true and whole. The total life of prayer is so vast and diverse that in this book we shall give attention only to a few of the most important facets of prayer.

God's Claim and Man's Surrender

No man enters the life of praying on his own initiative. The desire to pray is born of the Holy Spirit within us. Our initial motivations to pray may be very egocentric and selfish, but the Holy Spirit over the years will surely wean us away from such unworthy motives. The first work of the Holy Spirit is to lead us to Jesus Christ and to take of his life and ingraft him into us, wakening us gradually to the vast dimensions of Christ's life and power.

Our understanding and practice of prayer begin, therefore, when we are turned by the Holy Spirit to Jesus Christ as he has been portrayed in the New Testament. Here we are dealing not with scientific, disinterested biography but with the faith witness of those who loved him and confessed him as their Lord and Savior. We listen to their witness, and thus we expose our lives to the impact of Jesus Christ.

There we are confronted with the greatest personhood of all human history. We are faced with a personhood that towers high above every other person in history, a personhood radically different from what we find in ourselves or in any other person we know or know about. There we are presented with the true, full, perfect personhood that God intended a person to achieve. Christ's personhood was utterly free from any trace of egocentricity. His life had its center not in himself but in the Father. His selfhood was ever turned out from himself to an external reality which held absolute authority over him. He was glad to take up humbly the role of dependence and servitude to the Father. Christ's first words recorded in the gospels show his obedience to the Father already at the age of twelve:

> "Why were you looking for me?" he replied. "Did you not
> know that I must be busy with my Father's affairs?" (Luke
> 2:49).

And as his life ended upon the cross he revealed the same
attitude:

> ... and when Jesus had cried out in a loud voice, he said,
> "Father, into your hands I commit my spirit" (Luke 23:46).

The kingdom in Jesus Christ was the sovereignty not of
self but of God the Father. Set free from self-preoccupation,
he was therefore truly free to receive all that the Father sent
and to contain in his life the Father's life. Two lives joined
perfectly in him—the life of the Father and the life of true
manhood. Jesus' manhood was not at all like our sinful,
disobedient life but was true human life in the sense that God
intended man to live. For, as St. Francis of Assisi demon-
strated, we cannot have true human life until we are Christ-
indwelt and Christ-mastered.

When we look at ourselves, after looking at Jesus Christ,
we see a radically different picture of personhood. We know
that we are deeply and chronically self-centered. Egocentricity is a pattern of life we know from years and decades
of practicing it. No matter how far back we may go in
memory, we still find ourselves self-claimful and self-
centered.

By the time that we have reached even early adulthood, we
have built up over the years a large, rigid kingdom of the self
with myriad claims upon the world of objects around it. It is
from this kingdom of self and its self-sovereignty that Jesus
Christ would free us. The center of our life must be removed
from self and given to him. Egocentricity must be exchanged
for Christocentricity. Christ, as the agent of the Father in
creating us, knows long before we do that we were created
for God and not for self. He has the patience, wisdom, and

power to besiege our egocentric selfhood and transplant us from the kingdom of self into the kingdom of God.

It will require far more than a single brief conversion experience to achieve the transfer of sovereignty from self to Christ. The heart, or we might say ego, of man is desperately wicked and deceitful, and a siege, not a single decisive battle, will be needed to overcome that nature. We should therefore expect that the method by which Christ transfers the center of selfhood from us to him will involve a sustained, lifelong action.

The daily prayer of covenant with Christ, of surrender day after day to him, can be compared to God's use of snowflakes. I have for many years now called the prayer of daily surrender to Christ the "Snowflake Prayer." A single snowflake, seen through a magnifying lens, is very beautiful in design. No two snowflakes are identical; each one has individuality. Each snowflake is so fragile that one has only to breathe upon it and it is destroyed. But during winter storms and blizzards God dumps billions of tiny, weak, fragile snowflakes upon the higher levels of the mountain ranges where they build up a massive snowpack twenty or thirty feet in depth. The snowpack settles under its accumulated weight and at the bottom is compressed and congealed into solid ice. Loose fragments of granite rock lying on the surface of the ground are frozen into this ice. As the snowpack inches down the mountain, these rock chips become the chisel edges that God uses to grind down solid masses of granite rock into fine granules of sand, which the melting snows in spring will carry down the mountainside to deposit in river and lake beds. Hard granite is broken down by weak snowflakes.

So, too, God erodes man's hardness of heart by repeated use of the Snowflake Prayer of surrender. Said once or used only occasionally, the prayer is impotent. But prayed daily over decades of life, such a prayer effects mighty changes in our lives.

The words of the Snowflake Prayer are very simple, for the words that Christ through the Holy Spirit gives to us to use in praying are always simple words. As with all praying, there must first be a prelude to prayer. Let us first of all deal with this prelude. Our prayer of surrender begins not with our initiative but with Christ's prior action, claiming us for himself. Let us image him as invisibly present with us on our waking each morning, seeking to get our attention so that he may speak his words of claim to us. We do not see him present with ordinary vision, nor hear him speak as we hear human persons speak. It is with inner "seeing" and inner "hearing" that we meet him. He says to us,

> I am your Lord Jesus Christ:
> I was the agent of my Father in
>   creating you;
> I died upon the cross for you.
> Therefore, you do not belong to
>   yourself;
> you belong to me.
> Will you give yourself to me this day?

His words to us demand our response, and our response must always be freely given, never compelled. He allows us the terrible freedom to refuse to answer. Only out of thanksgiving for all that he has done for us over the years of our life do we willingly and gladly give him our answer:

> *O Lord Jesus Christ:*
> *In obedience to thy holy claim upon me,*
> *I give myself anew to thee this day;*
> *all that I am,*
> *all that I have;*
> *to be wholly and unconditionally thine*
> *for thy using.*
> *Take me away from myself, and*
> *use me up as thou wilt,*
> *when thou wilt,*

where thou wilt,
with whom thou wilt.

So much of our natural praying is an attempt to use God as a resource to do our will. This prayer is radically different. In it we daily give ourselves away to him. All of us are willing to be used in small part by God. But are we willing to be used *up* for his purposes, until we are left empty? Christ Jesus was used up by the Father. We too are to be used up by Jesus Christ for his purposes.

The Snowflake Prayer is essentially an early morning prayer. It may appropriately be prayed in bed on waking. Thus each new day of our life begins with the claim of Jesus Christ upon us and our acknowledgment and acceptance of that claim. If before we pray the words we first pause and hear his words of claim upon us, we shall not then pray the words lightly, routinely, or automatically. The prayer will be a response, not a reaction.

There will certainly come days when we do not *feel* like surrendering our lives to Christ. We may even feel like refusing to surrender. But is *feeling* our most important and trustworthy method of deciding? It is not at all dishonest or insincere or presumptuous on such days to go ahead and pray those words of surrender, for our praying is intended not only to express how we actually feel but also to impress on us how we ought to feel and obey.

The words of our conscious mind also have deep effect upon the subconscious levels of our being. The deepest resistances in us to the lordship of Jesus Christ over us are in the subconscious. The Bible speaks of the desperate wickedness which lies in the *heart* of man, but in the biblical view the heart is much more than the seat of the emotions, as we refer to it today. Perhaps the closest modern equivalent of the biblical word *heart* is *ego*, meaning the very center of a person's being. It is deep in the heart or ego of man that the issues of life are dealt with. Our prayer must therefore aim directly at those depths within us. Let me share with you a prayer which I have used for many decades:

> O Lord Jesus Christ,
> Take from me by loving force
> all that I withhold from thee,
> all that I will not give thee;
> and I am for thee, and against myself.

Gradually, hardly perceptibly, we become so attached to persons and things that we want to possess them as our own. Parents may so easily have possessive love for their children. Husband and wife may each seek to own the other and thereby stifle the other's life. We are so intent on owning things that we in turn become owned by them.

Our relationships to persons and things are intended by God to be very different, involving not ownership but responsible stewardship. We daily need to have our possessive hands pried loose from things and persons. Bedtime is perhaps an ideal time to do this. Then each night we relearn that our loved ones are ours on loan and not under ownership. Just as we belong first of all to Christ and not to the world, family, nation, church, or self, so we are to give up to Christ daily all the things and persons we want to own. After naming each of our loved ones, we can give them over into the hands of Christ by praying words like these:

> O Lord Jesus Christ:
> These loved ones are thine, not mine:
> I give them back to thee this night,
> for thy taking away this night in
>   death,
> or thy returning to me in the morning.
> Thank thee for the gift of them for
>   today.

By thus relinquishing them we do not lose them. Instead we enter into a new and very different relationship with

them. We free them from our inordinate attachment. Then
on the following morning we pray our thanksgiving to Christ
for entrusting those dear ones to our care for another day:

> O Lord Jesus Christ: I give thee thanks that thou art entrust-
> ing these loved ones to me for another day.

But this daily entrusting of loved ones to Christ will
depend upon the prior prayer of recognizing the lordship of
Christ over our own life. If we will not entrust our own life
daily to Jesus Christ, then we shall hardly dare to entrust the
lives of our loved ones to him. Entrusting oneself to Christ
entails that we also entrust our dear ones to him. Here, too, is
the very best preparation for the death of loved ones. If we
have daily given them back to Christ, to whom they truly
belong, then death is but the last such commitment.

Closely connected with our daily prayer of self-surrender
to Christ, and our submitting of our loved ones to him, is the
need for *pre*acceptance of each new day. We do not create or
order the day as we enter it each morning. The day is
presented to us by the mysterious providence and ordering of
Jesus Christ. He chooses the pattern of it, not we.

So much energy is wasted in the frustrations to which we
are prone when we are confronted with that which we do not
want. We resist, we detour, we complain, we try to escape
from much that the day brings—contacts with irritating
people, opposition to our plans by others, failure to accomplish what we had planned, or losing our temper. But if at
day's dawning we pray this simple prayer:

> O Lord Jesus Christ: I accept all that thou wilt bring me this
> day. Be thou sovereign Lord over every moment, every event in
> it.

—then we turn at once to Jesus Christ and rely upon his
proffered grace to meet every difficulty. We know that nothing can ever separate us from him and that he will deal rightly
with every event and crisis. Instead of fuming and complain-

ing, we quietly turn to him, look to him for guidance, and receive the grace to serve him.

Each person needs to translate the prayers he borrows from others into his own idiom. Until we have done so, our prayers are only secondhand prayers. The prayers here given as samples are those in my own idiom, which may not be yours. You may wish to borrow them for a time, but be ever on the alert to recast them in your own words. Over the years you will reach a way of saying them that satisfies. Then you will have found a home in the prayers, and as you go on using them they will not grow stale or lifeless. It is the work of the indwelling Holy Spirit to lead us gradually into words of our own idiom.

Prayer requires the use of words, inadequate as they may be. True, there is also wordless prayer, but we shall expect to use that kind of prayer when we are far more experienced in praying than we now are. We must be on our guard, for words can easily become merely noises.

What is the purpose of words? We take our inmost thoughts and mysteriously translate them into sound waves, which go out across space to another person who in turn will receive our sound-wave words, translate them into interior meaning, and so receive us into his life. Words are intended to carry and convey the gift of oneself to another. Yet how often this is not so! You may say the proper sound-wave words to the beloved: "I love you." Yet, hearing them, the beloved intuitively discerns that you are not in and with the words of your lips and says, "Now say the words as if you really meant them." It is the difference between a peck and a kiss. We are in the one, not in the other. When we turn to praying we often carry over with us our habitual manner of empty, hollow speaking.

Jesus' words were by no means empty, when he prayed or when he spoke to other people. In Matthew's version of the Gethsemane event, Jesus said to Judas Iscariot, "My friend . . . ." Jesus sought to give even to the betraying disciple the gift of his undying *agape* love and friendship. Those two simple words of address to Judas, "My friend," translated the inner friendship of Jesus for Judas into the form of simple words, which then crossed space and offered to Judas the gift of Jesus' unending love and forgiveness. Jesus put himself into the words of his lips.

In our praying of the Snowflake Prayer of surrender we shall ever have to face the danger of mere rote saying of the words. But that danger is no reason for not attempting to pray the words. Because we do not always truly give ourselves to our fellowmen in the words we speak to them, we do not therefore cease to talk with them. Whenever we are made aware by the Holy Spirit that we are merely saying empty words, let us pause, thank him for his loving correction of us, and then use the words rightly.

Praying that involves the hearing of Christ's claim upon us and our response of surrender is the cornerstone of all prayer. We are all too prone to seek God in prayer to use him for our advantage. We seek first not the kingdom of God but the kingdom of self. The prayer of surrender is an absolute necessity for any prayer life patterned on the life of Jesus Christ. Living for self must be replaced by living for Christ if we are to dare to call ourselves Christians. Only if we seriously and earnestly enter into this relationship with Jesus Christ can we expect that all other facets of prayer will be truly and significantly Christian. The prayer of surrender deals with the most crucial issue of sovereignty, and each of us must make a decision: Am I going to belong to Jesus Christ and serve him, or am I going to belong to myself and seek to use God for my own purposes?

Intercession

In our daily prayer of surrender to Jesus Christ we offer ourselves to him, in obedience to his claim upon us, that we may be used for his purposes. We know he calls us to conform our lives to his. Not only did Jesus love the Father with his whole being; he also loved all men and the whole world with the love that the Father showed him. Not only does Jesus Christ desire that we belong to him, as he belongs to his Father; he also wills that we come to have his own concern for the world. His concern for the world is expressed in his intercessory ministry for the world.

Too often, when we think of the ministry of Jesus Christ, we limit it to his incarnate years. We easily forget his pre-incarnate and post-ascension ministry to the world. The New Testament gives us a much larger conception of his total, eternal ministry than we often hold of him:

> He was with God in the beginning.
> Through him all things came to be,
> not one thing had its being but
>   through him (John 1:2-3).

> He is the image of the unseen God
> and the first-born of all creation,
> for in him were created
> all things in heaven and on earth:
> everything visible and everything
>   invisible, . . .
> all things were created through him
>   and for him (Colossians 1:15-16).

Of the post-ascension ministry, we read:

... He is living for ever to intercede for all who come to God through him (Hebrews 7:25).

He not only died for us—he rose from the dead, and there at God's right hand he stands and pleads for us (Romans 8:34).

Jesus Christ is the great intercessor. If we truly and deeply belong to him as Lord, day after day surrendering our lives to him, we shall receive the holy gift of becoming intercessors also. The life of intercession is not our achievement but a gift from Christ. Only he can re-create our lives so that we learn to follow the example of his interceding ministry. He wills to give to our lives two centers: first of all himself, and through him the Father; and, second, the world, because it is God's world.

Jesus Christ's post-ascension interceding is the continuance of a ministry which existed from the Fall and was made manifest to men in his incarnate years. We know that he was accustomed to withdraw from crowds and even from his disciples to be alone in prayer. At such times we may be certain that Jesus prayed not only for himself but also for the world, his disciples, and his enemies. His prayer from the cross is just one example of Jesus' prayer for his enemies. We are told that he prayed for Peter before the crisis which led Peter to deny him, and this was surely not the only time he prayed for Peter. In the fourth Gospel we find Jesus Christ's high-priestly prayer for his disciples. It is because we are so remiss in interceding that we find it difficult to understand the naturalness of Jesus' intercession. Our prayerless lives blind us to the majesty, depth, and power of Jesus' praying.

It is necessary at the outset to clear the ground of some widespread and erroneous conceptions of what intercessory praying is. Such widely held misconceptions are really but ludicrous parodies of what true interceding is. Intercession is not the giving of data, information, counsel, or advice to the Holy God. God does not need nor desire our counsel and advice. We can never give information to God, for he already knows all the data, and knows what he will do about it. Nor is intercessory prayer bringing pressure upon the Holy God to act, as if he were hesitant or reluctant to act. Nor again is it seeking to change the will of God by substituting our will. Much actual interceding certainly sounds like this, but it is not so that we ever see Jesus interceding. Jesus knew always that the holy will of his Father was not to be tampered with but to be learned and obeyed. We remember his prayer in Gethsemane:

> And going on a little further he threw himself on the ground and prayed that, if it were possible, this hour might pass him by. "Abba (Father)!" he said. "Everything is possible for you. Take this cup away from me. But let it be as you, not I, would have it" (Mark 14:35-36).

This was not at all servile resignation but instant, loving, obedient identification of his will with that of his Father, even when he could not comprehend it.

Perhaps we may best understand intercession by the use of analogies. Two such analogies are offered here to throw light upon intercessory praying.

Blood banks are familiar to everyone, and some of us have been donors of blood. In the blood bank the initiative is not with the donor of blood. We do not go about huckstering our blood. Rather the initiative is with the medical profession. It is they, not we, who are aware of the need for blood donations, and they make that need known to us. Recently an article on the front page of the San Francisco *Chronicle* mentioned the urgent need to replenish the meager blood-bank supply of the Bay Area. Within a day many people had responded to the need.

Made aware of the need by the medical profession we feel impelled to offer our blood to fill the need of others for it. We go to a hospital or blood-bank station and watch a portion of our blood drawn from our arm into a container. Very seldom do we actually witness the transfusion of our blood into the body of the recipient. We know that it will occur, not by sight but by faith in the medical profession.

Life, in the form of biological blood, has been transferred from us into another. We witness the mystery of the myriad interdependencies of lives. Another person lives because we have given ourselves, in the form of blood, into him. We are not permitted to give our blood directly into him. We might have the wrong type of blood or give it at the wrong rate. It must be given under the skilled ministry of a doctor or nurse.

Intercessory praying may be called spiritual blood donation. Intercession is the giving of self to Christ, the giving of life, love, and energy to enter the lives of others through him for their blessing. We give to them not directly but through Jesus Christ. Direct giving might often be harmful; but intercession through Jesus Christ always benefits the other.

As in biological blood donations, intercession begins not with our own initiative but with Christ's. Long before we become aware of the needs of others, Christ already knows and cares about them. He meets the needs of people by using us as the channels of his care. Through all of the modern means of communication—radio, television, telegram, letter, telephone, and newspaper—Christ is calling our attention to the needs of his children all over the world.

Today we know almost instantaneously what happens each day all over the world. How blind we all can be, failing to discern the action of the invisible Christ in all of these channels of communication. Through the television news report Christ shows us a wounded soldier in Viet Nam or the face of a frightened child or aged woman after a napalm bombing raid on a village. At first we see only outwardly in the ordinary way. But we may also receive from Christ the gift of deeper seeing or "insight."

A striking example of the two kinds of seeing is found in Mark's account of an incident in Jesus' ministry:

> He was preaching the word to them when some people came bringing him a paralytic carried by four men, but as the crowd made it impossible to get the man to him, they stripped the roof over the place where Jesus was; and when they had made an opening, they lowered the stretcher on which the paralytic lay. Seeing their faith, Jesus said to the paralytic, "My child, your sins are forgiven" (Mark 2:3-5).

All the others present saw the same externals—a paralytic lying on a stretcher. All had ordinary sight. But Jesus alone of all those there had insight. Looking upon the paralytic, Jesus with his deep sensitivity saw the loneliness and despair caused by sin. Here was a man separated by a great gulf of sin from the Holy God. Unasked either by the paralytic or by his four friends, Jesus closed that gulf and brought the forgiving Father into the paralytic's life by the simple words that he spoke, "My child, your sins are forgiven." There is not a hint that any of the others there were aware of the paralytic's deep need for forgiveness.

So too, as we watch news reports or read the daily newspaper we may simply see in the human sense, or Christ may give us insight. Christ mysteriously sensitizes our looking and observing. We find ourselves impelled to intercede for those at whom we are looking. Christ makes us care for them and give of our lives to them.

There are so many different kinds of spiritual blood transfusions that we may give to people whom Christ brings to us, if only we are surrendered to him. There are so many lonely lives to whom we may give not only our own human companionship but also Christ's. To tempted lives, weak and often defeated, we can bear witness to the mighty victories that Christ has wrought for us and so give them hope of victory in Christ. Into lives ignorant of who Christ is and what he has done we can bear witness of Christ's person and activity.

The whole earthly ministry of Jesus was occupied in offering spiritual gifts to men. He brought and gave to men the life of the Father, because he was so completely committed to the Father with his obedient life. So now the Ascended Christ would make use of our surrendered lives as the channels through which he gives the life of the Father to men today. We are taken up by Christ into his great intercessory ministry, to have our little share in interceding with him.

A second analogy of intercessory praying is grounded in the image-making faculty which God has given man. Imagination is the wondrous God-given power to make visible to the mind that which the eye cannot perceive. To imagine is to see what is invisible and nonsensory.

Using this power, we may imagine the great towering Jesus Christ, transcending our little world, looking at our world and at us, caring for our transformation into obedient sons of his Father. Our inner hearing understands his call, "Come." We come to him. We stand at his feet, so small before his towering greatness, looking up into his face and into his eyes. Then suddenly we realize that he is looking not at us but beyond and behind us. We feel the strong pressure of his hands upon our shoulders, making us turn so that now we stand before him with our backs to him. We look with him at the world, and as we do so, we find ourselves seeing much more deeply and penetratingly. Without any effort on our part, we receive into our lives his kind of caring for the world. We now see and care very differently than we did by ourselves. Something very mysterious is happening to us. He is entering with his life into ours; we are receiving him.

Then, above and behind us, we overhear him interceding for the world to the Father. The prayer that he prays is both familiar and at the same time utterly new, for it is the Lord's Prayer. At once we come under piercing judgment for our

mere reciting of his prayer, for the hollow emptiness of our
frequent misuse of his prayer. As we listen to him praying
that prayer, we are moved spontaneously and humbly to join
in and pray with him to the Father. Praying with him and
praying alone are two very different kinds of praying. We
learn anew to pray the Lord's Prayer by praying it with him.
He puts his words upon our lips and in our hearts. We sense
at once the fitness, rightness, and all-sufficiency of his great
prayer, for all of the Father's agenda for us in prayer is
contained in those simple, familiar words.

When Jesus gave his disciples the prayer which we call the
Lord's Prayer, he intended that they should pray these words
not only for themselves but also, perhaps more important,
when they interceded for others. It is significant that the
prayer uses not singular but plural pronouns. Nor did he
mean that these particular words, and no others, were to be
used. Rather he was giving them the agenda of God for
prayer. The Father's agenda begins, unlike so much of our
praying, not with petition and begging but with the name,
the kingdom, and the will of God the Father.

We all know how easy it is to recite by rote the familiar
words of the Lord's Prayer. We memorized it as children, and
both in common and in private praying we are apt to find
ourselves merely reproducing the sounds, rather than truly
praying. But we are confident that when Jesus prayed this
prayer he did not so recite it, for his whole life on earth
reveals how deeply he meant every phrase. He did not simply
say, "Hallowed be thy name," but gave himself in surrender
to the Father so that the Father might hallow his name in
him. He gave himself so that the Father's kingdom might
truly come in his life on earth. He surrendered his will to be
conformed wholly and unconditionally to the Father's will.
The words spoken by his lips carried the gift of his life to
God. So, too, Christ would have us pray, and not merely
recite, his great prayer. Then our praying will become conformed to his praying.

Because we are all prone merely to recite rather than to pray the words of the Lord's Prayer, we may find it helpful to take the agenda of the Lord's Prayer but paraphrase it in our own idiom. Here is an example of such a paraphrase:

> *Our Father:*
> *Thy name be hallowed in Viet Nam, where it is so terribly pro-*
>   *faned:*
> *reign over that war-torn land with thy Sovereignty;*
> *bend the many wills there until they are conformed to thy will.*
> *Give them day by day holy gifts of thy choosing;*
> *give them thy forgiving life, and enable them to forgive each*
>   *other;*
> *make them victorious in their myriad temptations;*
> *set them free from the terrible tyranny of evil.*

The structure and content are the same, but the words are in today's idiom. But we must take care that we do not limit ourselves to any single paraphrase of the prayer or we shall soon find ourselves once again reciting it by rote. But if we turn to Jesus Christ and let him give us the words in our own idiom, we shall find many such paraphrases. For family use we might pray his prayer like this:

> *Our Father:*
> *Hallow thy holy name in our home and family;*
> *reign over this home and family with thy good sovereignty;*
> *bend each of our wills until they are conformed wholly to thy*
>   *will;*
> *day by day make us to receive thy holy gifts, and do thou*
>   *choose them for us;*
> *make us to receive thy forgiving life,*
> *make us to carry thy forgiving life to each other;*
> *in our many temptations make us victorious;*
> *let evil and sin have no dominion or power over our lives.*

We are here confronted with a crucial decision. Do we really believe that when we pray, with or without words, something truly objective happens to the world? That there are subjective consequences of our intercessory praying is without doubt. When we intercede we drop for the moment concern for self, stop our chronic, unhealthy looking at self and turn outward to look at the world and at our fellowmen. Our horizons are stretched from the narrow and cramping world of the self into a vast world far out beyond us. Energy flows outward and is not kept dammed up within us. All this is very good for us.

But does intercessory praying go out across space and have an effect upon the world? Or would we do better to get out and take action—take part in a picket line, write a letter of protest to Congress, make a visit upon some sick or needy person? Would Jesus have better used his last days in Jerusalem by searching out blind and sick persons and healing them than he did by going into Gethsemane to pray alone? Was no real action taking place when Jesus prayed there? Indeed, the action taking place there in his time of prayer was probably the most important action of his whole lifetime and ministry, for our whole salvation is utterly dependent upon his obedient act of self-surrender to the Father which took place there. Interior action is just as important as exterior action, although men often shun the former because it demands so much more from them than do mere external acts.

When we intercede with Jesus Christ to the Father, a great interior action is taking place that will go out from us to affect the world and other people. We need no permission from men to pray. Jesus Christ is our sole and sufficient validation for such praying. What we understand about interceding will come after and because of our prayer.

We not only receive but also emit energy of many kinds. The divine life, which is a kind of energy, we constantly receive as *agape* love. We may also send forth this divine *agape* that it may enter into the lives of others.

Our humanistic culture has made us distrustful of all which we cannot analyze, dissect, understand, and control. We are intolerant of all that is mysterious. Yet it is an indisputable fact of human life that we are constantly being acted upon by powers and energies of which we are unaware. Intercession will always remain full of mystery, baffling our intellects. Nevertheless, there are questions we should raise. For example, what difference does it make when we are prayed for by others? Is there a difference only when we know that we are being prayed for?

A friend's daughter once told me, "Dr. Whiston, you do not know it, but for the past two years now a group of us young people, whom you led on a silent retreat to teach us to pray just before we went away to college, have been interceding for you and your ministry." I had had no inkling that she or they had been so praying for me. Now that I did know, I was deeply affected by the realization. But had there been no action upon me during those two years in which I was not conscious of their praying for me? Does the invading influence by others in our life begin only after we are made aware of what they are doing for us? Surely it does not.

In the years of our infancy and childhood, for example, our parents did much for us objectively of which we had no inkling, working upon us quite apart from any conscious understanding or cooperation? I thank the Lord that I know of well over five hundred persons who daily intercede for me. How many more pray for me of whom I know nothing? We are truly entered into by the intercessory praying of Christ-called persons and are fed by their prayers for us. Indeed, we are surrounded by a great host and crowd of witnesses, praying and working for us. We who are interceded for are upheld and strengthened by the loving prayers of others. And we know by faith that our prayers for others are not wasted but, in mysterious ways, will sooner or later aid and bless those for whom we pray.

We are not to demand instantaneous, pragmatic results from our praying for others. What pragmatic success did Jesus have as he hung upon the cross, alienated from his family, hated by his enemies, and deserted by his disciples? None. Yet he went on praying to the end. There would come a harvest from his praying for them, but only after his resurrection.

For whom shall we intercede? How do we find out for whom Jesus Christ means us to pray regularly? We cannot take a dictated list of names from him. We keep asking the question of him, "For whom wouldst thou have me intercede?" We find that names keep coming to us at odd moments along with the suggestion that we pray for them. Naturally we start with the names of people obviously given to us by Christ's providence—husband and wife, parents and children, friends, enemies, colleagues. We shall need some sort of notebook in which to jot down the names, for we dare not trust to memory. Too easily we forget many for whom we ought to pray. At first we jot down the names just as they come, but as the list grows—and it will grow—we may want to classify them: a page for our greater family, a page for the sick, a page for nations and their rulers, etc.

Praying for these persons requires a definite time and a definite place. It cannot be left to shifting mood or inclination. We may start by setting apart fifteen minutes as early in the day as possible. We may even rise fifteen minutes earlier to do this interceding before we breakfast. It may be done in our own bedroom or in the study, even outside in the garden if weather permits. Or we may take fifteen minutes from our lunch period, if we work in the city, and do it then—in a park or in a church which is open. It is Jesus Christ who invites us to come and meet him, keep a tryst with him and intercede with him.

It will be wise always to begin with a prefatory prayer, such as this one:

O Lord Jesus Christ:
In obedience to thy call,
I come unto thee,
to keep the intercessory tryst with thee;
to look up at thee,
to look with thee,
to receive from thee thy gift of caring,
to pray with thee for them to the Father.
Here am I.

Then we open our intercessory notebook. The names written in it are symbols which stand for real, specific persons. Seeing the written names reminds us of them, and we look at each person through the name. We do not need at all to inform Jesus Christ about this person; the Lord already knows in full. We do not need to compose a prayer for each person on the list. Rather we look with Christ at the persons, one by one, and as we do this we find that without effort on our part we are given to care for them. Then at the end of a group of names we pause and slowly pray with Christ a paraphrase of his great prayer. In fifteen minutes we may easily and without haste pray for several hundred people. There is no need to compose a separate and different prayer for each individual.

This way of intercession is not at all presented as the only way to intercede. It is humbly offered as a help until you, the reader, find your own particular way of interceding. Many persons have found this suggested way simple, helpful, adequate, and enduringly satisfying.

Shyness ever holds us enslaved in this matter of intercessory praying. Why is it that husbands and wives so seldom bear witness to each other that they pray for each other; parents for children, and children for parents; laity for clergy, and clergy for laity? One of our deepest spiritual needs is to know that we are cared for and prayed for by others. Life is very lonely, and we need this gift in that loneliness. We do not set out to tell everybody for whom we pray that we are praying for them. But when the sudden impulse comes to us to tell them, let us not squelch that impulse. It may be born of the Holy Spirit within us. A person may come to us to talk out his troubles. We listen. To listen humbly is a very real gift to them. But, if we are praying daily for him, we may also bestow upon him the gift of telling him so. Or in writing a letter to a loved one, we may at the end write, "Know that daily you are in my prayers."

Not always is it shyness, however, that prevents us from bearing this witness. More often we do not bear such witness because we do not intercede for them at all. To bear witness to any person that we pray regularly for him commits us to continued praying for him. And often when we let a person know we pray for him, it brings us as a gift in return his prayer for us. It makes a great intercessory fellowship of lives. It is by praying for others that we are prayed for.

Why is it that we are such inconstant intercessors? Why do our intercessory lists have such narrow horizons? Our pre-occupation with ourselves and those closest to us is very deep. We pray for our own nation, but do we also pray for other nations which may be our enemies? If we truly live in Christ and he in us, we shall move out from our narrow world into concern and care for all men everywhere. We do not intercede if we do not care. We will not care with anything more than selfish, humanistic caring unless we belong to Jesus Christ and receive from him his kind of caring. Then we shall become strong intercessors in fellowship with the Great Intercessor.

Vicarious Penitence and Confession

Our modern means of almost instant communication make us aware day after day of the terrible sins that man commits against man, the world of nature, and God. Daily as we read the newspapers we are face to face with the cruelties of men and nations—our diabolical instruments of war, our gross pollution of air, waters, and earth. Recent concern for ecology has made us more and more aware of what man has done to nature and thereby to himself and his future. Yet our protests so often lack any reference to God or to our sin against him. We are prone to condemn others for their wrongdoings—corporations, industries, criminals, radicals—forgetting that there is at the heart of it all a common guilt. Sin is never a private concern involving only the sinner. Our lives are so interconnected that all are implicated in the wrongdoing of any individual. We reflect this in holding parents legally responsible for the wrongs which their minor children may commit.

In my study I have a reproduction of Holman Hunt's great painting, "The Scapegoat," which I never tire of looking at. To grasp its meaning we need to read the passage in Leviticus which tells of the ritual of the Feast of the Atonement.

> Aaron must take the two goats and set them before Jahweh at the entrance to the Tent of Meeting. He is to draw lots for the two goats, and allot one to Jahweh and the other to Azazel. Aaron is to offer up the goat whose lot was marked "For Jahweh," and offer it as a sacrifice for sin. The goat whose lot was marked "For Azazel" shall be set before Jahweh, still alive, to perform the rite of atonement over it, sending it out into the desert for Azazel (Leviticus 16:7-10).

When the parents of Jesus took him up to Jerusalem to keep the Feast of the Atonement, Jesus must have witnessed this event. We can imagine him at some such time asking Joseph or his rabbi at Nazareth, "Can a goat really carry away the sins of men?" Perhaps Jesus pondered the great problem of what can take away the sin of the world.

In Holman Hunt's painting, we see a shaggy, long-haired goat on the shore of the Dead Sea. Across the Sea are the Arabim Mountains, from which Moses looked across into the promised land. The full moon, by which the feasts are set, is just rising over the mountains in the east. In the west there are storm clouds, the tail end of a severe storm. A short way from the scapegoat are the skull and horns of another goat. The scapegoat's front legs are about to collapse, and its hind legs are in an unnatural position, as if to prop up the body for a few more moments. The back is bowed as if it were breaking under an unbearable burden. This is the scapegoat from the Feast of the Atonement in Jerusalem, turned loose in the wilderness to carry away the sin of Israel. The High Priest transferred the sin of the people to the goat by laying his hands upon its head. Like Jesus Christ, the scapegoat will die in place of the people. No goat can ever take away the sin of the world, but God's obedient Son can carry away the sin of men.

In the Songs of the Suffering Servant of Jahweh, contained in Isaiah, we find still another example of the vicarious bearing of sin. The early church saw the passion and death of Jesus as a fulfilment of the Suffering Servant passages, particularly the fourth song in Isaiah 52-53:

> See, my servant will prosper,
> he shall be lifted up, exalted,
>   rise to great heights.
>
> As the crowd were appalled on seeing him
> —so disfigured did he look
> that he seemed no longer human. . . .

Like a sapling he grew up in front of us,
like a root in arid ground.
Without beauty, without majesty (we saw him),
no looks to attract our eyes;
a thing despised and rejected by men,
a man of sorrows and familiar with
    suffering,
a man to make people screen their faces;
he was despised and we took no account
    of him.

And yet ours were the sufferings he bore,
ours the sorrows he carried.
But we, we thought of him as someone
    punished,
struck by God, and brought low.
Yet he was pierced for our faults,
crushed for our sins.
On him lies a punishment that brings us
    peace,
and through his wounds we are healed.

We had all gone astray like sheep,
each taking his own way,
and Jahweh burdened him
with the sins of all of us.
Harshly dealt with, he bore it humbly,
he never opened his mouth,
like a lamb that is led to the slaughter
    house,
like a sheep that is dumb before its
    shearers
never opening its mouth.

By force and by law he was taken;
would anyone plead his cause?
Yes, he was torn away from the land of
    the living;
for our faults struck down in death.
They gave him a grave with the wicked,

a tomb with the rich,
though he had done no wrong
and there had been no perjury in his mouth.
Jahweh has been pleased to crush him
    with suffering.
If he offers his life in atonement,
he shall see his heirs, he shall have a
    long life
and through him what Jahweh wishes will
    be done.

His soul's anguish over
he shall see the light and be content.
By his sufferings shall my servant
    justify many,
taking their faults on himself. . . .

He was bearing the faults of many
and praying all the time for sinners (Isaiah 52:13—53:12).

In our imagination we picture the great, flat Babylonian plain, with a great host of mankind gathered together. On the horizon appears a small object, too far off to discern what it is. But as the object draws nearer it is seen to be a man carrying a huge burden upon his back. Bruised with scourging, he trudges along step by step. Our first thought is, "How this man must have sinned to be so afflicted!" We turn our face away, for we cannot bear to look upon him, so disfigured is he. Then from the crowd there comes a cry of a lone individual:

We had all gone astray like sheep,
each taking his own way,
and Jahweh burdened him
with the sins of all of us.

He was bearing the faults of many
and praying all the time for sinners.

Afflicted by God—yes, but for our sakes. It is God who laid upon him the unbearable burden of our sins. He willingly and prayerfully carries our sins away, and by his death we are healed.

The New Testament records the baptism of Jesus by John the Baptist. He who was himself without sin underwent, for sinners, the baptism of repentance for sins. He offered to the Father that which no sinner can ever offer: a full, perfect penitence and confession for sin. Sin always blinds, and no sinner, but only the sinless, can ever offer a satisfactory confession for sin. On the cross Jesus consummated his vicarious ministry of penitence and confession for all sinners, past, present, and future. By him the great gulf between sinful man and the Holy God is bridged, and now sinners may meet God face to face in Jesus, God's obedient Son.

But this vicarious ministry did not end with his ascension but continues until the end of the world. Christ now carries on that same ministry through the lives of men and women in whom he lives on earth. In their praying Christ still offers to the Father his vicarious penitence and confession. The sin of the world against God, not simply against man and nature, must be confessed. Today we have very little sense of sin against the Holy God. Many will not repent and will not confess. Therefore a few must do for the many that which the many will not do. Prayer must involve this facet of Christ's ministry.

We read in the day's paper of the killing of a policeman and the napalm bombing of villages in Viet Nam and Cambodia. Thousands of tons of lethal gas are dumped in international waters, despite the protest of U Thant of the United Nations. Entire blocks of city houses are demolished to build a freeway, leaving hundreds of poor people homeless. Stores are looted by a mob of irresponsible youths. Air, water, and earth are polluted, our own nation doing 56 percent of the damage. How easy it is to condemn those who do such things; but such loveless, uninvolved anger accomplishes no good. We leave God out of it all as if man's only offense were against nature.

Christ leads some of his followers to offer to God vicarious penitence and confession for these sins. The most important aspect of these matters is not what they do to man or nature but what they do to God. Man destroys what God created as good. Therefore, for corporations and industries, for criminals and vandals, for nations and races, we pray with Jesus Christ to the Father our prayers of penitence and confession. It is not "they" but "we" who have sinned, and our petition must be not to forgive someone else but to forgive us:

> Forgive us, the United States, that we have dropped atomic bombs on Hiroshima and Nagasaki and napalm bombs upon Vietnamese people and villages.

> Forgive us that we spend billions of dollars on space trips but let people live in dire poverty and in ghettos.

> Forgive this young man who under the influence of drugs has just murdered this policeman.

> Forgive us that our industrial firms dump their pollution into the Columbia River.

Some of these prayers of penitence and confession may be repeated day after day. Others may be prayed only once. But every day we will keep a trysting time with Jesus Christ which we devote to vicarious penitence and confession.

As we see with Christ, we shall come to identify ourselves with all of the world's sin, confess it, and in our little way offer God penitence for our corporate sinfulness. The world will be a very different place if some of us in it are daily engaged in this vicarious ministry of penitence and confession. This needs to be an integral part of the Sunday worship:

the minister should lead his people to look at mankind's grievous sin and to offer corporate penitence and confession. In this way the life that is in Christ Jesus lives in us, and we are conformed into his likeness as his ongoing ministry is lived out in us.

Thanksgiving

Thanksgiving is an essential facet of the life of Christian praying. The place it holds is an important index to our relationship with God. God is a God of giving, and all men receive far more from God than they acknowledge. It is a shame that the familiar words, "All things come of thee, O Lord; and of thine own have we given thee," are commonly applied only to the Sunday offering of money.

Giving thanks is a common experience. Escape from an accident, recovery from an illness, receiving an unexpected gift—all of these spontaneously evoke our momentary thankfulness. But seldom does the sense of thankfulness persist and endure. Soon the gift and the giver are forgotten as we busy ourselves with ordinary life. Moreover, we tend to give more attention to the gift than to the giver. Of ten lepers who were healed by Jesus, only one returned to give thanks to the giver. Nine knew only the gift; only one remembered both gift and giver.

Christian thankfulness is unique. It is much deeper and more abiding than merely humanistic thankfulness. We think of Jesus praying and giving thanks to the Father at a time when he had against him a united group of enemies, friends were abandoning him, and there were no signs of success. In that situation, he prayed, "I bless you, Father of heaven and earth, for hiding these things from the learned and the clever and revealing them to mere children" (Matthew 11:25). Remember Paul's words in the letter to the Ephesians, when he urges them to act in such a way "that always and everywhere you are giving thanks to God who is our Father in the name of our Lord Jesus Christ" (Ephesians 5:20).

Had Paul written, "giving God thanks sometimes for some things," we would say, "Of course." But Paul went much further than that; he thanks God even for times of suffering. In his letter to the Corinthian Christians Paul was goaded into recording for us a catalogue of the sufferings through which he had gone for Christ's sake:

> Five times I had the thirty-nine lashes from the Jews; three times I have been beaten with sticks; once I was stoned; three times I have been shipwrecked and once adrift in the open sea for a night and a day. Constantly traveling, I have been in danger from rivers and in danger from brigands, in danger from my own people and in danger from pagans; in danger in the towns, in danger in the open country, danger at sea and danger from so-called brothers. I have worked and labored, often without sleep; I have been hungry and thirsty and often starving; I have been in the cold without clothes (2 Corinthians 11:24-27).

Paul was no sadist. In later periods of Christian history we do find the practice of deliberate seeking after sufferings and also self-infliction of sufferings. But not a trace of this is to be found in the apostolic witness. Paul gives thanks to God not for the sufferings in themselves but rather for the communion with Jesus Christ he gained by willing acceptance of the sufferings. None of Paul's sufferings were self-chosen or self-sought. Centuries later in France a saintly Christian man, Fénelon, wrote to his friends living in the dissolute French court, "The crosses that men choose do not do the work of God."

It is usually only in retrospect that we discover the blessings God has given us in times of suffering. The sufferings themselves claimed our full attention while we experienced them, but long afterward we look back and discern what God did for us through them. We were not alone, and God was not far off. He was hidden in us, doing his mysterious work upon us although we knew it not at the time. Only belatedly do we then cry out,

O thanks be to thee, O Christ, for that which thou didst for me in that time of sickness.

O thanks be to thee, O Christ, for giving me that deep conviction of my own sin.

O thanks be to thee, O Christ, for that mighty humiliation and failure.

We give thanks to God for granting our requests, and we even thank him for refusing to give us that which we may have importunately demanded from him as a sign.

Let us look to our Lord's own life for an example of proper thanksgiving, for Christ's receiving perfectly matched the Father's giving. All that the Father appointed and gave, he received, and by his grateful receiving he made whole the Father's giving.

First of all, the Father gave him a loneliness that characterized his whole life and work. To whom could he turn for help, companionship, and understanding? There is deep pathos in Jesus' revealing words, "Foxes have holes and the birds of the air have nests, but the Son of Man has nowhere to lay his head" (Matthew 8:20). From very early in his public ministry Jesus was literally homeless, without understanding or support even from his mother and brethren. Down to the very end, his disciples were dreaming their grandiose dreams of the coming messianic kingdom and of their places of power and glory in it. Surely Jesus did not turn to three sleeping disciples in Gethsemane to ask for their help and strength. He had already foreseen and foretold their cowardice and treachery. He went to them, rather, to give to them his own watchfulness and prayerfulness so that they might meet the coming crisis armed by praying. It is because they were not watchful nor prayerful that they panicked, fled, and deserted their Lord.

Very early in his ministry Jesus became deeply alienated from his own family. Believing that their Jesus was beside himself, they sought to invoke the family authority to divert him from the ministry he was engaged in. He faced a united front of opposition in the religious leaders both of Galilee and of Judea. His own chosen disciples were not really with him, for they held very different conceptions of his messiahship than he held. One disciple betrayed him into the hands of his enemies. Peter denied even knowing him, and all twelve forsook him at the end. From the Father's own hands in the Garden of Gethsemane Jesus received the cup of passion, and he drank it alone. The highest Jewish tribunal condemned him to death, and Pontius Pilate handed him over for crucifixion. On the cross he met with railing and abuse. At the very end he had to receive from the Father the mysterious gift of being forsaken by him whom he had always served and glorified. Jesus could accept all these events from his Father because his life was anchored in the Father. The matter of prime importance for Jesus was not pragmatic success in the eyes of men but unswerving obedience to the Father.

In view of Christ's own experience, we must expect that following him offers no one a way of ease and protection from pain. We must expect to suffer if we follow him. We do not choose the sufferings that will come to us. Their occurrence will always be guided by the mysterious providence of God over us.

When we look at our own lives we find a sharp contrast to the life of Jesus Christ. We are so prone to escape or refuse suffering. When it comes to us nevertheless, we complain to God. How uncosting is the life of most Christians, laity or clergy. How far we are from the faith of Job, who said, "Though he slay me, yet will I trust in him" (Job 13:15, King James Version).

Let us look at three very holy gifts that Christ invites us to receive from his hands, and let us seek to gain some dim understanding of them as gifts. The first of these gifts is that of loneliness, a gift for which we never ask God but which he

is insistent that we receive from him. Again and again in life
we are made to be lonely. We can be alone even in a home, in
a group, in a crowd, in a church, or in a marriage.

What is God's purpose for us in loneliness? If we could
find satisfaction of our inner needs from within ourselves,
then we might well be content to lead a hermit's life. But we
soon learn that we cannot find fulfilment and satisfaction
within ourselves. The resources for building personhood lie to
a very large degree outside of us. Realizing this, we turn to
things outside us. If only we can find and get that, then we
will be satisfied, we think. But no matter how many things
we possess, we find that they are quite unable to satisfy us
within. If things could make people contented, then Americans should be the happiest of all people, and we are not.
Slowly we learn that we are not made for things. We then
turn to people. If only we can have friends and marry the
right person, then we think we will be satisfied. Yet, having
these, we find that no human love, however enriching and
blessing it may be, can fully satisfy the insatiable hunger
within us. God has made us to be a home in which he may
dwell, and our hearts are incurably restless until we find our
rest in him. This is the great promise and hope that is held
out to us in the conclusion of the whole Bible:

> I saw the holy city, and the new Jerusalem, coming down from
> God out of heaven, as beautiful as a bride all dressed for her
> husband. Then I heard a loud voice call from the throne, "You
> see this city? Here God lives among men. He will make his home
> among them; they shall be his people, and he will be their God.
> His name is God-with-them" (Revelation 21:2-3).

The invitation to loneliness comes to us again and again as
an invitation from God, that he may be with us and we with
him. Try as we may to escape loneliness, it returns to us
repeatedly. I ceaselessly thank God for the experiences of
loneliness that he has given to me. For in these recurring

times of loneliness my deepest experiences of God have come to me. God is found in things and in persons, it is true. But he also comes to us and finds us without such mediation. Although we may be in the presence of things and of persons, the invisible God can call us directly.

Men shun loneliness. Many escapes from it are offered to us in the modern world. We seek to escape loneliness by feverish activity, by turning on the television or radio, by reading newspapers or magazines, by cleaning out our desk, rearranging the furniture—anything that will serve to keep us occupied. Let us instead, when invited by God, enter into loneliness and welcome it as a time to turn to him and be with him. We can enter loneliness with a prayer such as this:

> O Lord Jesus Christ, do thou lead me into this time of loneliness, and do thy holy work upon me within it. Here am I; lead thou me.

We are not to ask for loneliness. It is Christ who chooses it for us. He knows our need for it and how to send it. And without this holy gift we shall never know Christ deeply. Blessed are the lonely, for they shall receive Christ in their loneliness.

The second holy gift from Christ, for which we never ask but which Christ is faithful in offering to us, is the gift of shame, guilt, and judgment. Every living person recurrently has such experiences. Have we ever realized that they come to us as the gift of Christ? We do much today to escape the experience of guilt and shame. Our consciences have become so hardened and callous that we are insensitive. We are right, of course, in avoiding a morbid and unhealthy kind of brooding upon shame and guilt. But we are blind to the rightful and wholesome use of such feelings.

One of the most terrible judgments ever pronounced on a city's people was that of the prophet Jeremiah. He knew intimately that city and all its people, high and low, rich and poor. He saw them through the eyes of his God and cried out several times in anguish, "These people know not how to blush." So accustomed had they become to the ways of evil that they had lost the holy power to experience shame.

Today we face the same danger. In the early part of the Second World War, we in the West were horrified at the terrible obliteration bombing of Rotterdam. Yet within a few years we were conducting much more deadly obliteration bombing, even to the extent of dropping atomic bombs on civilian cities of Japan, and we rejoiced at the victory we had won. More recently we have terribly defaced and ruined the good earth of the Creator in Viet Nam. What judgment does Christ make on our deeds?

Let us look more closely at the holy gift of shame and guilt. If we could sin and not at once feel shame and judgment, then we would have committed the "unpardonable sin" against the Holy Spirit: that we are totally insensitive to the Holy God. Christ and the indwelling Holy Spirit are ever faithful. The moment we sin, we experience the presence of Christ with us in redeeming judgment. We do not ask for shame and guilt but, on the contrary, have every reason not to want these gifts. Yet Christ gives them to us without our asking. He knows we need them, and therefore he gives them to us.

We should rejoice that we are able to experience shame and guilt in his presence, for by that we know we are sensitive to his holy life and can respond. Let us at such moments not try to escape this experience but unashamedly pray our prayer of thanksgiving for the gift of shame.

> *O Lord Christ, thanks be to thee, that thou hast given me this most holy gift of shame and guilt. Do thy holy work upon me through them. I receive them from thy hands.*

Then we shall know the peace of acceptance and forgiveness, not the morbidity of brooding. So long as we are able to experience shame and hear the words that conscience speaks within us, we should rejoice and be glad. We are sensitive and responsive to the Holy God.

The third holy gift, for which we never ask but which from time to time Christ sends us, is the ministry of bearing pain. Jesus Christ calls us to follow him in the way of redemptive suffering. The apostolic witness clearly interpreted the ministry of Jesus Christ as that of the Suffering Servant of Jahweh. Is this ministry of Jesus limited to the incarnate ministry of Jesus, or is it also a part of the post-ascension ministry of Christ through his body the church? Are not we as members of that body also invited to be pain-bearers for his sake? St. Paul writes of bearing in his own body the sufferings of Christ. Let us seek to understand something of this gift and ministry, even though it will always remain a mystery.

We can best grasp it, not by abstract thinking but in a concrete event. I once visited a woman, a stranger to me, who was hospitalized in a large urban medical center in the terminal stages of melanoma cancer. She had lost both of her eyes to the dread disease. When I first met her she was in almost continuous pain. Holding her hand, I could feel the pain throbbing through her body. She was given periodic doses of morphine for relief from the excruciating pain. She asked me to read to her from the Bible about the passion of Jesus, and, while her husband also listened, I read to her from the Gospel of Mark. When I had finished, after a moment of silence, she asked me to read it again, and I did. Just then the doctor and a nurse entered the room. It was time for another injection of morphine to alleviate her pain. Quietly she said, "Doctor, I have a request to make of you." "What is it?" he asked. "That you permit me *not* to take the morphine this time."

All of us were startled into sheer silence by her request. Then the doctor replied, "No, you must take the morphine. You cannot possibly bear the pain without it." Again she made her request, in a voice both quiet and firm. "Doctor, please grant me this request." The doctor, the nurse, her husband, and I were in deep silence. We knew but did not fully understand that something very deep, mysterious, and awesome was taking place. Finally the doctor said, "Yes. But you have only to touch the call-button and the nurse will come instantly and give you the morphine." Then the doctor and the nurse left the room. Her husband and I remained silent. After some moments she spoke to me. "Do you know why I made that request of the doctor? In the passage you read were the words, 'They offered him wine mingled with myrrh, and he refused it.' I knew at once that he was inviting me to refuse the morphine and enter deeply into the pain."

When I returned the following day she had just died, and for the last twenty hours of her life she had taken no injections of morphine but had endured constant pain such as few people could bear. But just before she died, she spoke two prayers in the presence of her husband.

Lord Christ, I entrust my husband and our two children to thy care,

she said, and after a moment of silence, she added:

Lord Christ, I give myself to thee.

Had she been under the influence of the morphine she would probably not have uttered those two great prayers as a dying gift to her husband. She had accepted and obeyed a mysterious calling from Christ to glorify him in her pain. Who of us can dare to say that she was mistaken and deluded?

There is a great tide of pain in the world, pain which appears to have no connection with individual guilt. This pain has to be borne. It cannot be escaped, and Christ often calls his own to stand firm in the face of evil and pain, by his grace bearing it and thereby glorifying him. Neither the husband of the woman mentioned above, the doctor, the nurse, nor I can ever forget how she glorified God in her deep pain during those last hours of her life.

We must not seek out pain. That would be sadism, and there is no place in the gospel for sadism, self-inflicted pain, or inflicting pain upon another. We shall of course make use of all the gifts of medicine to alleviate pain and suffering. Yet we cannot deny that there is a mysterious vocation of pain-bearing. St. Francis of Assisi, in the later part of his short life, knew pain intimately; he addressed it as "Sister Pain." St. Francis' deepest praises for his Lord came from the midst of Sister Pain's visitations.

Surely the forgiving father in the gospel parable knew pain and suffering more deeply and truly than did his prodigal son. Did he not agonize over his son's waywardness? An essential part of the prodigal son's re-creation of what he had destroyed depended upon his realization that he had caused his father to suffer by what he did. The forgiving father was a suffering servant.

Prayer must always be guided by the knowledge that God's choosing for us is far wiser and more redemptive than ours. So often we ask amiss. We ask that life be made comfortable for us, but Christ requires that we be faithful and obedient. In preaching at the ordination of one of my students, I stated that Christ would surely call his servant to suffer for his sake. Afterward the student's father and mother complained to me that they did not want their son to enter into suffering. They wanted him to be spared that. I could only reply, "Your son cannot follow Christ and not be called upon to suffer."

Christ chooses for us. We receive all that he mysteriously appoints for us. Perhaps a radical paraphrasing of the clause in the Lord's Prayer dealing with God's giving needs to be prayed constantly:

Our Father: I will receive whatsoever holy gifts thou dost choose for me this day. By thy grace I will trust thee, and obey and serve thee.

We need to restrain our readiness to complain against God's providence over our lives. So often we voice our distaste for what Christ appoints for us. We prefer to ask and choose rather than to receive and obey that which he chooses for us. We need to learn from Job, until with him we cry out, "Though he slay me, yet will I trust in him."

Not only in the great, climactic events of life are we to give thanks but also in the commonplace, seemingly little things. In our chronic self-reliance we are prone to think that we can get these things for ourselves. Thanksgiving, in that case, seems utterly irrelevant. Let us have a second look at this.

We waken each morning into another new day. When we retire at night we take it for granted that we shall awaken in the morning. But can we really be sure that we shall waken to another day of life? Can we keep ourselves in being? No, each new day is a gift from God which we do not earn at all. We can learn much from the prayers of the past.

Since it is of thy mercy that another day has been added to our life, . . . who hast safely brought us to the beginning of this new day . . . (The Book of Common Prayer).

It is easy to begin a new day without praying. But if we pray, we enter the day thankful to God for the gift of it. The air we breathe, the water we drink and bathe with, the food we eat, the ability to see, hear, smell, touch and feel—all these are gifts to us from God. I would share with you a waking prayer that I have used daily for decades:

O Lord Jesus Christ:
Thanks be to thee

for watching over me through the night
hours,
protecting me from all danger and evil,
and bringing me in safety to the gift
of a new day,
in which to live for thee and by thee
and in thee.

It makes a tremendous difference if we begin the day in the mood of thanksgiving to God.

It is a most humbling experience to sit down and record all the happenings of a particular day in a long list and then ask of each item, "Did I remember to give God thanks for this?" Our list may remind us of the ministry to us of the telephone operator, the airline, the mailman, the refuse collector, the policeman, the sales clerk, and an unexpected friend for tea.

All of these things we too often "take for granted." It is a shame that that phrase has come to have such a casual meaning. To grant is to make a gift. "To take for granted," therefore, is "to receive a gift." But we are so insensitive to God's continuous giving to us through countless different channels that we fail to discern him as the ultimate giver.

Remembering always that prayer has two foci, both God and man, we need to undertake the ministry of vicarious thankfulness on behalf of others who do not thank God. We do for them that which they are too blind to do for themselves. How many remember to give thanks to God on their safe arrival at an air terminal? I have this custom of praying my thankfulness, not only for myself but for all the passengers:

O thanks be to thee, O Jesus Christ, that under thy mysterious
providence thou hast brought all of us in safety to this airport.
We thank thee for the ministry of this crew and for all those who
watch out for our safety in travel.

Or, as we drive on a freeway, we notice the highway patrol-
man aiding a stranded driver. We watch a man helping a blind
man across a busy city intersection. In happenings such as
these, Jesus Christ calls us to offer thanks to God that God
has raised up such people.

As we grow up in Christ, more and more we shall receive
the gift of being thankful to him for all things, great and
small. We shall find ourselves caught up in the ministry of
vicarious thankfulness for the unthankful. One of the marks
of our growth into distinctively Christian prayer will be the
decrease in petitions for the self and the increase of thankfulness. Thankfulness will prepare us for the life of heaven, to
join that great fellowship who are forever praising and thank-
ing God.

Praise and Adoration

Thanks be to God that there are some things in his universe that man can put to no use. They are good only for what they are, not as a means to some other end. We lift up our eyes and the rainbow confronts us. We see the full moon rising over the eastern mountains, reflected on the waters of a lake. We gaze in sheer wonder at the glory of the sunrise or the sunset, and we know what the Psalmist meant when he addressed God as "thou that makest the out-goings of the morning and evening to praise thee" (Psalm 65:8b, in *The Book of Common Prayer*). So constantly do we live in the kingdom of means, where everything exists for the sake of something else, that it is freeing and blessing when moments come to us when we can live in the kingdom of ends, where things are good for their own sakes.

Let us call to memory observing a glorious sunset sky. First of all, we are set free from preoccupation with self. We forget self, so rapt are we with the glory and beauty of the sunset sky. We are also given the gift of silence, and our chattering ceases. At such times words are unwelcome intruders. We are quite content to be still and gaze at the sunset sky. The desire to use dies instantly. We have no desire to own the sunset, to copyright it, to make a profit from it, or to use it for any purpose. It is an end, not a means to some other end.

We realize, when we reflect, that it is not so much we who act upon the sunset as the sunset that acts upon us. We are content to be in the passive, receptive mood, a welcome vacation from our chronic activism. There is nothing we can do for the sunset; there is much it can do for us. The sunset gives us beauty and glory such as man can never make.

Peace steals into our disturbed lives, and cleansing takes place. We cannot have an unclean or selfish thought as we stand gazing at the great panorama of color and form in the sky. It does not seem right to have the experience all alone. We call to another, "Come, look!" Unselfishly we want to share the experience. Our whole being is lifted to a new dimension. We act as a whole person; our interior schisms quietly disappear. There is probably no person living who does not at some time have this adoring experience, in it knowing that life is good to hold such a gift. Our response to such moments is spontaneous and impulsive. We become for the moment a new person; and it is very good.

Yet when we pray, we are hardly in the presence of God but we bring out our shopping lists and inform God what we want. In relation to God we are like professional beggars, wanting God to serve us. We treat him as a means to our ends. He is good *for us.* God certainly intends that we come to him with all our needs and voice them, and he knows that the fulfilment of our lives lies in him. But surely God also desires that there be times when we come to him not for what we can get from him but solely for his own sake. Is this not true in our human relationships? We want our neighbor to feel free to come to us to borrow something or other. But if the neighbor comes to us only on those occasions, we resent it, for we feel that we are being treated as a means to her ends. God desires that there be regular times when we come into his presence, with no shopping lists in our hands but desiring just to be with God.

So accustomed are we to self-seeking use of God, that this adoring, non-utilitarian relationship with God cannot be left to chance or mood. It must be practiced if it is to become a stable part of our total prayer life. We must consciously will to adore God. Gradually, adoring of God will become as natural as breathing; but in the beginning stages begging will often supplant adoration.

God desires that we adore him, not for his own gain but for ours. God knows the peace and joy that will come to us when we adore him. Prayer of adoration is one of his most holy gifts to us. True adoring prayer will at first require effort because of our chronic egocentricity. The angelic beings praise God, and if we are to be made inheritors of that world we, too, shall need to be adorers and praisers.

It is perhaps the Orthodox Churches who most emphatically manifest this note of praise and adoration in their anthems and prayers. The worshiper is turned away from himself to gaze at God and his glory. The Psalter also is full to overflowing with this invitation to praise and adore.

> *We worship thee, Lord, in the beauty*
> *of holiness;*
> *Let the whole earth stand in awe of thee.*
>
> *Blessed art thou on the glorious throne*
> *of thy kingdom:*
> *Praised and exalted above all for ever.*
>
> *O all ye works of the Lord,*
> *bless ye the Lord:*
> *Praise him,*
> *and magnify him for ever (The Book of Common Prayer).*

One of the most perfect, pure prayers of adoration is the familiar Sanctus:

> *Holy, Holy, Holy,*
> *Lord God of hosts,*
> *Heaven and earth*
> *Are full of thy glory:*
> *Glory be to thee,*
> *O Lord Most High. Amen.*

In such prayers of adoration and praise, the personal pronouns referring to ourselves drop out. We efface ourselves completely. They are wholly concerned with God, and although it is we who are the adorers no mention is made of the self. Many of the Psalms as we know them have been rewritten to refer to God in the third person, since they are spoken to fellowmen about God. The Psalmists undoubtedly thought of God originally in the second person. Thus, we read in Psalm 19,

> The heavens declare the glory of God; and the firmament showeth his handiwork (King James Version).

The original experience was probably expressed in direct address, as follows:

> *The heavens declare thy glory, O God; and the firmament showeth thy handiwork.*

When we speak directly to a person, we call him not "he" but "thou" or "you." Prayers of praise and adoration, in pure form, are in the form of direct address. We may even select passages from the Psalter or from a hymnal, recast them into direct form, and use them as our prayers of adoration.

Prayer of praise and adoration will bear fruits, but that is not their purpose. The fruits are additional gifts from God which come to us unsought. Little by little, as we praise and adore, we are set free from our egocentricity. Playing the role of object worked upon by God, rather than subject acting upon God, our lives become dominantly theocentric and therefore healthy and whole. It is the pattern of life for which God created us. We turn our backs upon the hellish kingdom of means and move toward the kingdom of ends, where God dwells. We are being prepared by God for heavenly life, in which our feverish straining to own and use will be replaced by joy in God as our central goal. The Franciscans called it "the secret of naughting."

Unless we regularly practice adoration it will not become part of our life of prayer. The acts are at first to *im*press in order that later they may *ex*press. We need to learn to become adorers. Even before our waking prayer of self-surrender to Christ, we might first pray to him in adoration rather than petition:

> *Praise be to thee, O Jesus Christ.*
> *O Christ, thou art the Lord.*

Such prayer should be very brief. A very few simple words will suffice, followed by moments of wordless silence in which we gaze in wonder at the invisible Christ. From such adoring we then pass into the holy business of hearing the claim of Christ upon us and making our response in the prayer of surrender. If we truly desire to become an adorer for Christ's sake, the Holy Spirit will prompt us to do it upon waking each morning.

We should not limit our adoring prayers to the beginning of the day. We need to say such short prayers throughout the whole day. All of us have moments between the tasks of the day in which our attention could be turned to Christ in adoration. While we wait for the traffic light to change, while we wait for the next person to come into our office, whenever we look at our watch—we can use this fleeting moment in which to adore Christ. It is done interiorly. Nobody else will even know we are doing it.

It is helpful at first to link up adoration with something which we do frequently, so the doing of the familiar act will remind us also to adore. Fénelon taught some of his friends at the French court to turn to God in adoration whenever they heard the clock strike. We might do so whenever we glance at our watch. When we waken in the night hours, we might then utilize the waking moments to adore Christ.

We have to start wherever we now are. Pick a recent day and go through it hour by hour as you can remember it. Were there moments in it when you turned to Christ, not asking anything from him but just rejoicing in him? How frequently did this happen? As the years pass by let us become less and less beggars from God and more and more adorers of him.

Devotional Reading

The life of prayer will not grow deep and stable unless it is regularly and repeatedly fed. For biological growth we require regular meals each day all through the years of our life. Our spiritual growth and health similarly depend upon daily feeding upon the right diet. This will require the practice, day in and day out through the years, of devotional reading.

Authentic Christian life has always been nourished deeply and regularly upon the Holy Scriptures and the devotional classics. Our age is characterized by a growing ignorance of both. Even in theological circles, teachers and students are more prone to read books about the Bible than to read the Bible itself. While books of theology require some basic knowledge of the time and condition which produced them for proper understanding, biblical writings and the devotional classics are as nearly independent of history as books can ever be. Time matters little to them. They partake of eternity and are not dated or outmoded for those who read them many centuries later, for they contain elemental and essential truths for men of all ages.

A former professor at Harvard wisely counseled a group of clergy:

> There is nothing necessary to an understanding of the life of Jesus which may not be had by anyone who will read the Gospel of Mark in the King James Version with open eyes (Sperry, *Strangers and Pilgrims*, p. xv).

We read the Bible and the devotional classics not by the framework of church history or systematic theology but in the light of our own personal Christian experience. We read not only with the critical intellect, but with heart and will and mind—the whole person.

The reading of the Bible and devotional classics is a unique kind of reading, very different from quickly skimming the daily newspaper. Baron von Hügel wrote that this kind of reading is as unlike our ordinary reading as the slow dissolving of a lozenge on the tongue is unlike ordinary eating.

We might take an analogy here from farming. In the spring the farmer plows, harrows, and fertilizes his fields. Then he casts in the seed. He knows that much time must elapse before the seed will germinate, develop a root system, and finally appear above the ground and slowly grow into a mature crop. The farmer must wait patiently for the harvest to come. The process cannot be hurried up but goes on at its own pace.

By contrast, our reading is often done impatiently. We want instant results. We fail to realize that the reading we do today is like sowing, and the harvest may come years later. Nothing is wrong if in our day's reading no harvest comes to us. We must learn patience from the farmer. The harvest will come in God's own time if we are faithful in sowing.

A second analogy may be taken from the hearing of music. We go to a concert and hear a great orchestra play a concerto. As we return home we realize we have not exhausted all that the music contains. At times our attention wandered and we really heard only parts of it. So we may buy a tape of the same concerto and play it in our own home. Each time that we listen to it we hear something new. Each time we hear it as a different person, and new notes in it strike our attention. That is why we never tire of hearing it.

So it is with Bible reading. It is familiar material, yet we know that it contains very much to which we have never wakened before. There is nothing automatic in the coming of new insights, but when least we expect they seem to break through to us. It helps also to use different versions of the Bible, giving the familiar renewed freshness.

We need to read in a prayerful mood. We should always begin such reading with a prayer, to remind ourselves of what we are about to do. There is a great difference between devotional reading done with precedent prayer and that done without it. I share with you my way of doing this in the hope that it will encourage the reader to do the same in his own idiom:

> *O Lord Jesus Christ, in obedience to thy call, I come to thee. Do thou place me humbly at the feet of thy chosen servant, St. Mark, that being taught by him I may meet thee, hear thee, understand thee; to surrender my life to thee, to serve and obey thee.*

The prayer reminds one that what we are seeking is not an abstract religious idea but a personal meeting with Jesus Christ. Then, with this preamble, the actual reading begins. Such reading needs to be done very slowly. Modern techniques of rapid reading are quite out of place here. We read almost effortlessly. Any touch of strain is self-defeating. One is alert and receptive but not demanding.

Openings and insights will come when and where Christ chooses to give them. We wait patiently for their coming, perhaps for years. When God speaks to us in what we read, then we stop and let ourselves be carried by the words. I may be reading, for example, the words spoken to Peter by Jesus on the night before he suffered, " . . . I have prayed for you, Simon, that your faith may not fail . . . " (Luke 22:32). I may find that Jesus is speaking not only to Peter but to me, and my name replaces that of Simon in the text. Then I know that I have a strong intercessor who will never give up his claim upon me. Such openings will be unique for each person who reads. What was originally merely historical thus transcends history, having the mysterious power to span the centuries and speak directly to us today and so become living words of a living Christ today.

When these openings come it is essential that we express our thanks for the gift from Christ to us. It is not the cleverness of our keen intellects that has ferreted out this truth. Rather it is a gracious, unmerited gift from Christ. To receive the gift is not enough; it must lead us into a relationship with the giver of the gift. We might express our thanks in a prayer such as this:

> *Thanks be to thee, O Jesus Christ, that thou hast met me and spoken to me in these words.*

Then it is helpful to underline the words or make a marginal notation to remind us, in future rereadings, of the words that have brought about these meetings with Christ. Another helpful practice is using the blank pages in the back of the Bible to index such passages. Dividing the pages into sections for the letters of the alphabet, we may record the words that have come alive. Suppose I have been reading the passage in Mark 2 telling of Jesus healing the paralytic, which we quoted earlier. The insight comes to me that here is a clear case of Jesus' giving forgiveness before it is asked for, in the absence of any sign of penitence or of confession. We normally expect forgiveness to follow repentance and confession. So under the letter *F* I record, "Forgiveness, Mark 2," and under *R* I note, "Repentance, Mark 2."

Such entries will over the years become one's own, personal, living concordance of Scripture passages, very different from the objective concordances of scholars. Here is the record of God's meeting and speaking to one directly through the Bible's words.

Our devotional reading need not be confined to the Bible. Through the centuries gifted saints have written the great Christian classics, which have much to give us if we will sit humbly at their feet and receive. Through them we keep company with the saints of Christ. We need to open our lives to theirs and let them teach us, witness to us, lead us, and tell us their experience of the riches of Christ. Christ has given me much through long years of reading Augustine, Francis of Assisi, Thomas à Kempis, Fénelon, Francis de Sales, Olier, Charles de Condren, and others.

The reading of these classics, valuable as it is, is no substitute for reading the Bible. It is a supplement, not a substitute. In every great classic of devotion the author points us back to the Bible and to Christ. The classics must not be given only a single reading. Rather we need to saturate our minds and memories with an author, reading and re-reading over a period of years. Each time we return to a work we discover much to which we were blind before.

We sorely need a disciplined method of devotional reading. If we leave it to impulse, inclination or mood, it will be done irregularly and may die out entirely. There are certain daily acts which we do with habitual regularity—eating meals, reading the paper, opening mail. Let us link up our devotional reading with these regular habits. We will not look at the newspaper, let us say, until after we have done our reading in the Bible and one of the Christian classics.

We do this reading not from compulsion but because Jesus Christ desires to have us do it, that he may daily meet us and give himself to us in it. Our obedience is not to a rule, but to Jesus. For his sake we may decide to rise fifteen minutes earlier and do this devotional reading very early in the day.

Over the years we will reap a rich harvest from such devotional reading. We feed our lives regularly upon Jesus Christ through this reading, and he becomes for us a real and living presence despite his invisibility. We find ourselves growing in spiritual wisdom and power. We are made whole in Christ. He makes his home in us, and we know what it is to have our home in him.

Part III

THE RELEVANCE OF PRAYER

The Christ-izing of Life and Work

If prayer is limited to those times which are specifically set aside for praying to God, then the largest part of our life will be unrelated to God in prayer.

The Greek word *atheos,* which gives us our English word "atheist," applies far more widely than we are accustomed to think. We have tended to use that word only of those who expressly deny that God exists. The word actually means "without God." Whenever and wherever we live with no conscious reference to God, then we are living atheistic lives. For the vast majority of people both life and work are largely atheistic in this sense. God is deemed quite irrelevant. What relevance can God have to an engineering problem, to repairing a plumbing leak, to servicing an auto or airplane?

Every person begins his life wholly atheistic, that is, with no conscious relationship with God. God always has a relationship with us, whether we are aware of it or not. The goal of life is heavenly life, wholly theistic life in which every moment and event is consciously related to God. Somewhere between those two points stands each of us now. As the years and decades pass by, are our lives becoming more and more theistic or increasingly atheistic?

Our chronic, sinful independence leads us into deeper and deeper unrelatedness to God. In the six hundred years since the Renaissance we have all been subtly brainwashed by the humanist credo: that man is the measure of all things, that he is intended to be self-reliant, and that there is almost no limit as to what he may accomplish for himself. Our present world condition is the dire harvest of this humanistic period of history. Humanistic living and theistic living are radically different.

More and more the work that men do and the life they live are unrelated to God, and without prayer both work and life are joyless. As you wait in airports and observe the faces of travelers, very few of the faces that you see could be truly described as joy-filled, radiant, peaceful. What you see are jaded, jittery, fatigued, joyless faces. When you travel the beltways that encircle our great metropolitan areas, you see very attractive factory and office complexes with beautifully landscaped grounds and attractive architecture. It appears that these must be truly delightful places in which to work. But go there again at the end of the working day. Watch how quickly the workers get into their cars and speed away, and observe the tense, tired faces of so many of them. The vast majority of workers in office, shop, factory, or store find no joy in their daily work. They have a job but not a ministry or vocation.

It is tragic that the word "minister" has come to denote almost exclusively the ordained ministers of the church. Every man's work should be a ministry, given him by God to serve and bless his fellowmen. The lawyer, the doctor, the housewife and mother, the gas station attendant, the refuse collector, the policeman and fireman, the politician, the telephone operator, the airline crew member—each has his unique ministry to perform under God to bless people. It is *prayer* in one's work that will change a job into a ministry.

For many years now I have had a friendship with an airline captain on the trans-Pacific run of one of our major airlines. I was once visiting in his mother's home when he and his wife called to report that he was about to resign his position as a pilot. When his mother asked him why, he replied, "I know no joy in the work. I am fed up with it."

"What do you want to do then?" asked his mother. He replied, "I do not know." I asked him if he would postpone his decision to resign for a month and try an experiment. The experiment was this: As he was seated in his captain's seat with his fellow officers in the cockpit of the plane, after checking all the instruments, he would do one more act. He would turn inwardly to the invisible Christ and "hear" him say,

> Will you be my minister of aviation, and fly this valuable plane, its cargo, and these people to Tokyo for me?

He would reply,

> *I give thee myself, to be thy minister to carry these people, this cargo, and this plane to Tokyo. Here am I; use me.*

On arrival at Tokyo, before leaving the cockpit, he would have this prayer:

> *Thanks be to thee, O Christ, that by thy grace I have been enabled to bring the plane, cargo, and people safely here.*

Some ten years have passed since that day, and my friend is still a jet pilot. His work is not a joyless job but a joy-filled ministry, simply because the work has been related to Christ in prayer. What has happened to him can also happen to every other worker. A school teacher can take a few moments before her pupils arrive to sit at her desk and thank Christ for entrusting the students to her ministry for the day. The lawyer or doctor can offer himself to Christ, just before the client or patient enters his office, to be Christ's minister to him:

> *O Christ: thou art bringing this person to me, to use me to minister in thy name to him. Here am I; use me.*

The housewife and mother is occupied day after day with what are often looked upon as monotonous chores: preparing meals, washing, ironing, making beds, dusting, tidying up rooms, shopping for food. To wash and dry and put away dishes three times a day every day of the year over several decades can certainly be joyless work. Here every wife and mother needs to know Brother Lawrence and learn from him. Brother Lawrence, a lay Carmelite brother in a house in Paris, had the menial work of a kitchen helper. He tells us that amidst the confusion and clutter of the noisy kitchen he carried on a running conversation with God, just as much as he did in the hours set apart for prayer and worship in the chapel.

A mother wakes at dawn and at once must begin preparing breakfast for her family. As she goes to the kitchen, let her think of Christ claiming her for his minister:

> Will you be my minister to this man and these children, and prepare for them my gift to them of daily bread?

She may reply in prayer:

> *Here am I, Lord Christ: use me.*

Then as she prepares the food, she may do exactly the same things she has always done but now do them for Christ's sake. St. Paul gives us the same counsel: "Whatever you eat, whatever you drink, whatever you do at all, do it for the glory of God" (I Corinthians 10:31).

After her husband has gone off to work and the children to school, then Christ calls the wife and mother to the next task.

> My world is one of order and beauty and cleanliness. Will you be my minister to wash these dirty dishes; make up these beds, tidy these rooms; do the dusting?

And she again replies,

> *Here am I; use me, O Christ.*

Thus the day is spent in a series of little ministries, given by Christ and done to serve and please him. Work is no longer lonely work, because every task is done in the presence of the invisible Christ.

The office worker on his way to work may intercede for his colleagues and coworkers. The telephone operator may rejoice in knowing that Christ uses her to connect lives for the purpose of talking.

I ask the reader to make a very revealing self-examination in this matter. Rule a sheet of paper into three vertical columns and about thirty-six horizontal lines. The three vertical columns are headed "Time and Use," "Related to Christ," and "Unrelated to Christ." Then take a recent day in your life and in the first column begin by writing down the hour you wakened. Then divide the day into half-hour periods until your sleeping hour. In each half-hour period record briefly the main use of that time. Then think again of each half-hour and ask yourself if what you did in it was in any conscious way related to Christ. Put an X in either the second or third column. Finally, add the number of X's in the second and third columns, and you have an idea of just how central Christ is to your daily life and work.

Faced with the many portions of our day which are not yet centered on Christ, we need to proceed patiently and prudently. Take one activity at a time and try to remember to relate it to Christ, slowly forming the habit of praying in connection with it. When that activity has become Christ-centered undertake another project. We do not accomplish these tasks ourselves; rather, we become open to receive them as a gift from Christ. He calls us, and we receive.

Gradually more and more of our waking day becomes centered on Christ, and we have the deepening companionship of Christ in all that we do. If there is anything that we do about which we cannot rightly pray, we should drop it from our life. Christ desires to be our Lord in all that we do, so preparing us for the life of heaven when all shall be related to God.

Prayer and the Family

One of the most serious symptoms of the sickness of our society today is the widespread breakdown of family life. The rapidly growing divorce rate and the widespread practice of extra-marital sexual intercourse must be of deep concern to every earnest Christian. In the history of man the death of a culture has often been accompanied by the breakdown of the established sexual relationships.

The life of prayer must be relevant to family relationships between husband and wife, between parents and children. We cannot assume that wife and husband pray for each other, or that parents pray for their children or children for their parents, for such prayer is increasingly rare.

Many people who seldom darken the doors of any church still turn to the church to celebrate their marriage ceremony. In some forty years of ministering to those who have come to me for help with marriage problems, I have never found a couple who recalled having received any instruction in prayer as part of their premarital preparation. Yet marriage is a relationship in which we most sorely need the help of Christ in prayer. Far too many people enter marriage on the precarious foundation of romantic love alone, thinking of their union in a sociological rather than a theological light. The clergy who solemnize marriage have a unique opportunity to offer significant guidance in prayer to the couple who enter this new dimension of their lives. Moreover, if the minister fails here, there is no other institution that will take up the task.

Marriage is the entrusting by Christ of two persons into each other's hands. It is the gift of entering deeply into each other's life. Marriage therefore is a ministry and vocation

118

under Christ, whether we are aware of this or not. And just as prayer is an essential part of entering into marriage, so also continued development of a marriage will require prayer, daily renewing the vows of marriage. In my forty years of ministry Christ has taught me much and corrected me often in the matter of prayer and marriage. Let me share with you some of the insights that I have found to be helpful for many couples. Regardless of whether or not the couples ever used the suggestions of prayer which were offered them, yet they were offered this gift.

Prayer must deal, first of all, with renewal of the marriage vows. Wedding vows cannot be a once-for-all affair. Unless they are renewed regularly, marriage vows will easily wither and die. Nor is an annual celebration of the wedding day enough. Daily it is necessary to renew in prayer the marriage vows. My own way of doing it is this:

> *O Lord Jesus Christ:*
> *In obedience to thee,*
> *I pledge anew my sacred troth*
> *to love this thy child in thee;*
> *make us one in thee forevermore.*
> *I give thee myself,*
> *my body and my lifeblood,*
> *for her most holy blessing,*
> *peace,*
> *joy,*
> *freedom,*
> *fulfilment, and*
> *companionship.*
> *Receive me, Lord Christ,*
> *purge and cleanse me,*
> *rule and order me, and*
> *make us one in thee forevermore.*

In this daily prayer we accept anew each morning Christ's claim to use us in the ministry of marriage.

Even in marriage, we all have a shyness at the deepest levels, and prayer is at the deepest level of all. But if one daily renews the marriage vows in prayer, then the day may come when husband or wife may dare to break through this shyness and renew the troth directly to the other. Waking would be an appropriate time for this, and each could say to the other:

> *Beloved:*
> *I pledge thee anew my sacred troth,*
> *To love thee in Christ*
> *this day and forevermore.*
> *I give thee myself,*
> *my body,*
> *my lifeblood,*
> *for thy most holy blessing,*
> *peace,*
> *joy,*
> *freedom,*
> *fulfilment,*
> *and companionship.*
> *Receive me, beloved, and*
> *by thy receiving make my giving whole, and*
> *make us one in Christ forever.*

The reply might be like this:

> *I receive thee, beloved, and*
> *I thank our Lord Christ, and*
> *I thank thee,*
> *for the most holy gift of thee.*

We cannot blithely assume that the foundations of marriage will grow firm. The pressures of evil today are widespread and pernicious. All of us need the armor of prayer as our defense.

Along with this waking act of renewing vows might be added other prayers such as these:

O Lord Christ, thanks be to thee that thou hast watched over us all through the night hours, keeping all danger and evil far from us, and brought us into the gift of this new day, to live together for thee, with thee, and by thee.

We accept all that thou wilt bring to us this day, Lord Christ; be thou our sovereign Lord in every moment and event in it.

Following these two prayers husband and wife might well pray aloud together their daily prayer of surrender:

O Lord, Jesus Christ:
In obedience to thy claim upon us,
we surrender our lives anew to thee
        this day;
all that we are,
all that we have;
to be wholly and unconditionally thine,
for thy using.
Take us away from ourselves and
use us up,
as thou wilt,
where thou wilt,
when thou wilt,
with whom thou wilt.

If Jesus Christ is to be the living Lord over marriage and home, we shall daily need to expose our lives to him. Never can we know enough of him. To *know* in the biblical sense involves far more than factual knowledge; it requires self-giving to him. In the Old Testament the word used for knowledge of God is the same term that is used of sexual intercourse. To know my wife is not simply to know how tall she is, the color of her eyes and hair, what she likes, and such data. Rather it is to give myself to her and to be received into her life. To know Jesus Christ, then, means to give oneself to him and to receive him into one's own life. Accordingly, there should be a daily time, perhaps as short as ten minutes, when husband and wife sit down together, open the New Testament, and read a short section. By this daily reading together, of the gospels in particular, husband and wife are daily confronted by the invisible Lord Jesus Christ. Mutual giving to and receiving from that Christ are then possible.

Lastly, it is more rewarding to pray the Lord's Prayer together aloud, perhaps recasting it to apply to one's marriage and home:

> *Our Father:*
> *Hallow thy name in our home and marriage;*
> *reign over our home with thy sovereignty;*
> *bend our two wills, and make them one,*
> *conformed wholly to thy will:*
> *make us to receive only what thou dost*
>   *choose for us this day;*
> *make us to receive thy forgiving life,*
> *use us as carriers of thy forgiving life*
>   *to others;*
> *make us victorious in our temptations;*
> *set us free from every evil power.*

All of these early morning devotions need not take more than twenty or thirty minutes. Our lives are very busy with too many things, and the beginning of the day tends to be rushed and hurried. But if we deem our relationship to Jesus Christ truly important, we could rise a half-hour earlier and have time to do this.

Bedtime is another appropriate time of prayer. So easily marriage becomes a possessive relation, and each wants to own the other rather than give himself in love. We speak of "my wife" or "my husband," yet it is only Christ who has the right to own persons. We need to recognize through prayer that we have one another on the basis of Christ's daily giving:

> *O Lord Jesus Christ:*

We thank thee for the gift of our
   love this day;
now we give our love back to thee,
for thy keeping, or
for thy returning in the morning.

Thus we are reminded daily that giving to each other in marriage is based upon Christ's daily giving, not upon any right of ownership.

What if one of the partners in marriage is unwilling to pray in this way? Then the willing one must pray alone, for self and vicariously for the other, ever hoping that the day may come when it can be done mutually.

These prayers together are not intended to be a substitute for one's own private praying. Each person remains an individual, and there will always be an area of absolute privacy, known only to God, in our praying. We need both private and mutual prayer.

It is sad indeed that sexual relationships are so often utterly unrelated to God, the creator and giver of sexual joys. The intimate relation of ecstatic joy in sexual union is a most holy gift of God. It is far more than a merely biological experience. Today both literature and films confront us frequently with a sordid degradation and perversion of sex, and we must oppose this trend.

We are unmistakably taught in the New Testament that the human body is a temple in which Jesus Christ can dwell. What we do with the body, therefore, we do to Jesus Christ. Too much sexual union really expresses lust, not love, and even in marriage lust is ever present. Love must battle lifelong with lust. Here again prayer can be a mighty weapon to ensure that sexual union be under Christ's sovereignty. Christ gives a wondrous gift of oneness and union, not directly but mediated through one's partner in marriage. A prayer such as this may express it:

O Lord Jesus Christ:
We offer our bodies to thee,
that by their union
we may be thy instruments
to bring each other
thy holy gift of joy and oneness.
Here are we; use us.

After the act of union we may pray,

O Lord Jesus Christ:
thanks be to thee
for the holy gift of ecstasy
thou hast given to us
through our bodies.

Such prayers will deepen and sanctify the mysterious act of sexual union. Husband and wife will know that they are engaged in far more than a means of self-gratification. They will know that their union is truly a sacrament, a ministry of Christ to fulfill each other.

Again, prayer needs to be closely associated with the miracle and mystery of procreation. Where sexual intercourse is intended for procreation, a prayer such as this may be used:

O Lord Jesus Christ:
We offer to thee our two bodies,
that by their union
thou mayest use us
in thy creation of a new life.
Here are we; use us.

Then, when conception has taken place, the wife may pray daily,

O Lord Jesus Christ:
I give thee my body,
that from it

thou mayest use us
in thy creation of a new life.
Here am I; use me.

Prayed daily through the months of pregnancy, such a praying ministry can mightily bless both mother and baby. With the birth of the infant, a prayer such as this could be used:

O Lord Jesus Christ:
We give thee thanks
that thou hast entrusted to us
the care of this new life.
Lead thou us
in the life of parenthood,
and use us to lead this thy child to thee,
to confess thee as Lord and Savior.

With the coming of children, prayer as a family begins. Family life today is so deeply fragmented and so busy that it is difficult to make place for life together. Family prayers have become the exception, not the rule, even among church people.

The mother is the first teacher of prayer to her young child of four or five. After the father has gone off to work, her little child will learn from her daily praying for the child's father. At first the child simply observes and listens as the mother prays aloud, perhaps the Lord's Prayer, for the father:

Our Father:
Hallow thy name in Daddy this day;
reign over his life with thy
  sovereignty;
conform his will wholly to thy will:
give to him this day holy gifts of
  thy choosing;
give to him thy forgiving life,
use him as a carrier of thy forgiveness
  to others;

make him victorious in his temptations;
deliver him from every evil power.

The child may not understand the words. But a powerful impression is made upon the child's memory by witnessing his mother in the act of praying. As this is repeated day by day, the child will join in on a few of the words, and finally he will be able to recite the whole prayer. The habit of daily praying for his father is being implanted in the child. Gradually intercession can be extended to include the child's playmates and relatives. The mother is teaching by her example the practice of intercessory prayer.

Father, mother, and children must also join together in corporate prayer. It need not take up much time, perhaps as little as five or ten minutes. Perhaps before rising from the supper table, the family may first read a short passage from the gospels and then pray in unison the Lord's Prayer in the traditional words or in paraphrase:

Our Father:
Thy name be hallowed in this family;
reign over us with thy sovereignty;
bend our wills to conform to thine:
give to us day by day holy gifts of
    thy choosing;
give to us thy forgiving life,
enable us to forgive each other;
make us victorious when we are tempted;
deliver us from every evil power.

Thus every day the gathered family is made to remember the invisible Jesus Christ.

Just because of the invisibility of Christ it is helpful to have in every room of the home some visible token of Christ's constant presence. It may be a simple cross, a picture, or a religious symbol of some kind.

The family must also worship together in church, joining

with others who belong to Jesus Christ. It will do no good to send the children to church school on Sundays while father and mother remain home. The children need the visible witness of their parents engaged in worship together with the parents and children of other families, praising and confessing Jesus Christ.

Books also play an important part in the growth of prayer life in the family. At first father or mother may read to the children, but as the children are able to read themselves they should be given books about Jesus and the Bible itself so they can be helped to form the daily habit of devotional reading. I remember when my mother gave me a copy of the Bible on my twelfth birthday and made me promise her that before retiring each night I would read a chapter. It was the beginning of a fifty-eight-year habit of Bible reading, and I bless her for her wisdom in that. Biblical illiteracy is widespread, and the life of prayer to an invisible Jesus Christ will not long endure if it is not rooted in the habit of daily Bible reading.

As the children grow up they will inevitably rebel at times against family prayers. One cannot compel such praying. The children must have the freedom not to pray. But then it is all the more essential that the parents regularly and visibly continue the family prayers, bearing witness to the rebellious children that they consider such praying important. In this way the children may eventually be won back to participation in family praying.

Without prayer, communication between husband and wife and between parents and children too easily becomes peripheral and shallow, and it may even end altogether. Prayer opens the way for deeper giving and communication between family members. Shyness and lack of real communication is perhaps the most serious and most common failure in family life today. We know a person deeply only when we are free to pray for him and with him.

Prayer and Sickness

Vast numbers of people in our culture are afflicted by physical, mental, or spiritual illness and are desperately searching for healing. Not only individuals but also groups—families, corporate groups, and nations—are critically sick. Many of us are old enough to remember the very beginnings of the healing movements in this land, within the churches and outside them. Today they are widespread and common. The rise and rapid growth of the psychological sciences is telling evidence of the dire mental sickness of our time.

An ancient adage says, "Sickness is a visitation of the Lord." In our skeptical, sophisticated age, we so easily deride the aphorisms of our forefathers. But we ought to show more respect for the accumulated wisdom of the past generations. In every sickness, regardless of its origin, God is actively involved and concerned.

This is not at all to say that every sickness is a judgment from God. There will always remain a mystery in the cause of sickness. Who would presume to explain why this person comes down with deadly cancer, or why this child is struck down by an auto and crippled for life? Yet we cannot doubt for a moment that God is present in every case of sickness or accident. God does visit the sick, seeking to fulfill his holy purposes with them. In many cases we can see that God sends sickness, not arbitrarily but through the laws governing health. We neglect the cleaning of our teeth, and God sends pain to warn us and lead us to the dentist for healing. Every sickness, major or minor, is an invitation to turn to God and receive that which he chooses for our good.

When we make a call as a Christian friend upon a sick person, whether in a home or in a hospital, we need to prepare for the call by prayer. While driving to the hospital or home, we need to be reminded through prayer how to minister to the sick person. We might pray in this way:

> O Lord Jesus Christ, I give myself to thee to be thy minister to this sick person and his family. Do thou give me thy words to speak, that I may be used of thee to turn him to thee for the receiving of those holy gifts which thou art seeking to give him. Here am I; use me.

We do not make the call in our own name but go as the minister of Christ. The sick person's real need is not for us but for our Lord Jesus Christ. We go not simply to make a social call and talk of peripheral matters. The sick person expects a Christian friend to bring him into the presence of Christ, to speak words from Christ, and to bring him graces from Christ. If we fail him in this, we fail him grievously. Why are we, both laity and clergy, so shy at dealing openly with the things of God? Why do we talk such small talk at such times, not knowing what to say or pray?

The answer is not to look up ahead of time an appropriate prayer in some book of prayers. Perhaps we should heed the penetrating judgment of the Clinical Training Directors, who counsel their trainees *not* to pray with the sick. For reading a prayer from a book of prayers or reciting a prayer from memory may not be real prayer. Unless we visit the sick as men of prayer, perhaps we should not pray at all.

But if we truly know God from long years of regular, disciplined praying, if it is natural to us to speak to the invisible Christ, then we are not free not to pray. We *must* pray. We need not ask the sick person, "Would you like me to say a prayer for you?" If Jesus Christ gives us the impulse to pray, then we need no other cue nor anyone else's permission.

What is it that the sick person expects from us in prayer? Usually it is a prayer for his healing, for quite naturally he seeks through us the healing action of Christ. But must we always give that which they desire and choose? One of the collects in the *Book of Common Prayer* reminds us that God "giveth us better things than we desire or pray for," and even in times of illness we often ask wrongly. Our total communion with Jesus Christ will give us the right agenda and the right words to speak in prayer. We are the instruments through whom Christ comes, speaks, gives, and claims.

Early in Jesus' Galilean ministry he healed the paralytic at Capernaum. What the paralytic and his four friends desired was the healing of the paralytic's body. They asked nothing more. Yet Jesus gave first of all something which none of the five asked for—forgiveness—for that was what the Father wanted the man to receive. We, too, must become sensitive through our life of prayer to that which God would give to the sick.

A doctor in a little-known Swiss sanitarium used to make the rounds of the patients each morning, saying the same prayer each morning with each person:

> *O God, if this person will glorify thee more by being healed, use us here for his healing.*

This prayer we can all accept. But this wise and sensitive doctor added:

> *O God, if this person will glorify thee more by remaining sick, let him remain sick.*

This two-sided prayer reveals the heart of the issue: are we using God for our purposes, or is our main purpose to offer ourselves to God?

Consider Jesus' own example, recorded in John's Gospel, when he healed the man born blind. The disciples asked the wrong question: "Who sinned, Lord, this man or his parents, that he was born blind?" Jesus replied, "Neither he nor his parents sinned. . . . he was born blind so that the works of

God might be displayed in him." The glorification of God, so confounding to our neat rationalizations of God, must concern us even more than health. For we may be physically and mentally healed and yet not a whit nearer to being an instrument to glorify God.

Let me share with you the sort of prayer I have often used in visiting the sick, whether at home or in the hospital. Taking the person's hand, I pray:

> *O Lord Jesus Christ, whatever thy mysterious purposes may be for this sick person, and for his family, grant that he may accept them, obey thee, and by thy grace glorify thee.*

Healing is certainly one of the purposes of God, but he may have immediate purposes other than healing or in addition to healing. By such a prayer we avoid trying to limit God to our own narrow horizons.

Sickness is always an invitation from God to turn to him and give him our attention. So often in our busy living we have too little time to attend to God. In illness God gives us time and opportunity to be still and know that he is God. Are we so preoccupied with our agenda with God that we do not heed his agenda for us? Sickness gives us time to turn to God and listen to him.

It is often said that in praying for the sick we should have no doubts, for God always gives healing. Conditional praying—"If it be thy will . . . "—is really faithless praying, this view holds. But the New Testament confounds every attempt of man to make such rigid restrictions on praying. Jesus gave us both the injunction to believe we have what we pray for and the example of his own conditional praying in the Garden of Gethsemane:

> *Abba (Father)! Everything is possible for you. Take this cup away from me. But let it be as you, not I, would have it* (Mark 14:36).

Jesus was not inconsistent here, and we must follow both his command and his example. Our natural, impulsive desire for the sick one is for his healing. Having that desire, we can be honest in our praying only by articulating that specific desire for healing. We bring to Jesus our deep desire for healing of our loved one and place it confidently into his hands. Having done that, we trust him, even when we cannot understand what he chooses to do with our desire or with the sick person.

"If we have sufficient faith, then God will always heal," it is said. But who is to judge how much faith is sufficient? Did St. Paul have insufficient faith when his thrice-repeated prayer for Christ to take away his affliction was refused? The father of the epileptic boy cried out, "I believe; help my unbelief." No prayer could be more honest or more paradoxical than that, but does the fact that his prayer was granted mean that his faith was greater than Paul's?

Think of the blind beggar at Jericho, seeking alms from the pilgrims on their way to the feasts at Jerusalem. He may have been a lifelong beggar, crying to all who pass, "Have mercy on me!" Jesus passed by and he cried out, "Jesus, Son of David, have mercy on me." Probably on every prior occasion when someone asked, "What do you want me to do for you?" he had habitually replied, "I want money." But this time he impulsively cried out, "Lord, that I may receive back my sight." Perhaps the words were no sooner said than he was puzzled and asked himself, "Why did I not ask for money? What I have asked for is utterly impossible."

Jesus discerned faith in this impulsive petition. Convinced that God had put this daring request upon the beggar's lips, Jesus responded by giving from his Father the gift of healing. Grace poured out upon grace! Faith, we see in this parable, is our response to a prevenient action of God within us, often causing us to act in an unusual manner. Each response to

God's prevenient grace opens the doorway to further acts of grace.

We must be so sensitive to God and his prevenient action upon the sick that we become the channels through which he gives further grace. Our faith response is always as much of a surprise to us as to others who see it. We cannot plan it or prepare for it. It seizes us and we respond.

We need to examine carefully the motivations behind our desire for healing by prayer. Why do we want to be healed? What will we do with our life if we are healed? Will our relationship to God, the world, and our family be one whit different, once we are healed? The healing we ask for turns out in many cases to be spiritually sterile. It would bear no harvest of truer, deeper, more dedicated living for God or for man.

Sickness gives us much time which cannot be filled with the usual activities of everyday living. Through hours and weeks we must wait. What work of God needs to be transacted in this period? The sick person finds himself alone with God. Thoughts, memories, and judgments come unsought. They seize our attention and make us come to terms with God concerning the past and the future. When God comes to us he comes as a purging fire, but with the burning come peace and remaking. Forgiving accompanies judging. In illness we take a deep spiritual inventory and thus gain piercing self-knowledge. Far more is involved than self-judgment and self-acceptance. We receive the gift of acceptance by God, and we no longer have to deal with self-acceptance. Without acceptance by God we would need self-acceptance, but self-acceptance alone would be futile and frustrating.

By its very nature, sickness tends to turn a person in upon himself and thus deepen egocentricity. A deep need therefore in times of sickness is to be turned out from the self toward God and other persons. When we visit a sick person, we can be of great help by suggesting he use his time to intercede for others. Doctors, nurses, interns, orderlies, roommates, other patients in the hospital—all need to be prayed for. This outgoing tide of energy often seems to speed the inflow of health into the sick person. While he is quietly and peacefully turning to God and interceding for others, the healing work of God takes place within him.

Prayer also has a real relevance for the doctor, the clergyman, and the healed person once the sickness is over. Here so often both the doctor and the clergyman fail by default. The sick person has been healed and is now back at home and back to work, but the event of sickness is not really over. There should be a most important sequel, one which we cannot just take for granted, of thankful prayer for the gift of God's healing. The healed person, moreover, must endeavor to live more closely to God in home and work than before; where sickness has been due to disobedience to God and his laws, repentance must be made and forgiveness received.

Has the healed person made a new covenant of obedience to Christ? We need to heed the warning that Jesus spoke to a healed person in Jerusalem, "Sin no more, lest a worse thing happen to you." Something very important would be added if the doctor, the clergyman, and the healed person and his family would meet together, recognizing in talk and in prayer that God gave the healing through the doctor and nurses as his channels. The clergyman, in any case, should not miss this important opportunity to bring God into the foreground of the healed person's life. "How will you show your thanksgiving to God for his healing?" he may ask. "Will you come to the Eucharist and, in our Christian fellowship, offer public thanks for your healing? Is your thanksgiving so deep that it will manifest itself in regular worship in the church and in private praying?"

Not all sickness ends in healing. Some is chronic, lasting over years and decades. Christ invites one suffering from chronic illness to accept the very special ministry of serving, obeying, and glorifying God in sickness. But this will be possible only with the support of deep, sustained praying. Here is a daily prayer that may be used:

> *O Lord Jesus Christ, I accept this new day as thy gift to me, to be used in spite of sickness and pain to serve thee, obey thee, and glorify thee. Here am I; use me.*

Chronically ill persons may be used by God for the important ministries of intercessory praying and vicarious penitence for the sin of the world, thus taking an active part in the church's ministry. Such a ministry of prayer can turn these persons away from the crippling imprisonment of self-pity and self-preoccupation and give them joy in serving Christ and man. Those who are well have a ministry to the sick; and the sick also perform a ministry to the rest of the world for Christ's sake.

The most certain fact in life is death. We meet it first of all in the death of those known and dear to us. Sooner or later, we know, death will come to us. In our praying we need to prepare for the coming of death, both to our loved ones and to ourselves.

We prepare for death in our nightly surrender of ourselves and our loved ones to Christ, letting ourselves be reminded each night at bedtime that all belong truly to Christ. Christ gives us a day-by-day entrustment of life.

Sick people often desire to die. They know that they are a burden to those who attend them, and they see no purpose in life. Loved ones, too, may desire that an afflicted person depart and be freed from his crippling, incurable sickness. I was once called to minister to an aged man who for some years had been bedridden in the home of his son. As we talked together, he confided that each night he prayed God to take him in death. Why should God continue his useless existence on earth day after day?

There is always a mystery, far beyond our understanding, in sickness and death. I suggested to him that he pray this simple prayer each morning:

> *O Lord Jesus Christ:*
> *I accept from thy hand*
> *this gift of another day of life.*
> *Do thy holy work upon me in it.*
> *I do not understand;*
> *I trust thee and thy wisdom.*

At the end of each day, I suggested that he pray, instead of a plea for death, words such as these:

> *O Lord Jesus Christ:*
> *I give thee back this day*
> *which thou didst give me.*
> *I give myself to thee this night,*
> *for taking away this night in death,*
> *or for waking again tomorrow.*
> *I trust thee and thy wisdom.*

In such praying we fall back upon the mighty, mysterious providence of Christ over our lives. Our small intellects can know only a very small fragment of Christ's plans for our lives. In our prayer, let us recognize that there is much we cannot understand, and let us place our trust in Christ, who knows all. In his will is our peace. The loved ones who watch day by day over the sick may pray in the same fashion.

Finally death does come, and at such a time we need to ground our lives deeply in prayer. Except in cases of prolonged illness with no hope of meaningful recovery, we have an almost instinctive desire to recall the person back to life. The desire is quite natural, but we know that no return from death is possible here.

A lady whose husband had been killed in an airplane accident just a week previously once came to me with her teen. I asked her to pray after me these simple prayers:

O Lord Jesus Christ:
I accept this tragic death of my husband,
and I give thee thanks
for the twenty-two years
thou didst entrust him to my loving care.
Now I entrust him to thy never-failing
    care and love forever.

O Lord Jesus Christ:
Do thou lead me into this
new life of bereavement;
interpret to me its holy mysteries,
and use me as thy servant in it
to bless other lives.
Here am I;
use me.

Another Christian widow took up the ministry in her small town of visiting every widow to pray with her and befriend her. We can find deep peace even in the midst of loss and sorrow if only we will turn to Christ. He cares for our loved ones far more than we do. Christ is always to be trusted, even in the darkness of death.

The School of Prayer

One of the basic laws of spiritual life is that, once having received, we must give or we will lose what we have. We learn best by having to teach others. Every teacher knows that it is in the process of teaching his pupils that he learns his subject best. If we have received from Christ the gift of the life of prayer, we feel impelled to seek that others, too, shall receive this gift.

The last three decades have witnessed the birth and rapid growth of an institution which was formerly unknown: the school of prayer. Most such schools have arisen at the initiation of laymen.

We live in disturbed times when nothing seems stable and everything is in flux. Anything may happen. When old securities are taken away, men seek desperately, often blindly, for true security. When earthly realities betray and fail us, men seek to find the heavenly realities which do not change or die but abide forever. Prayer is one such reality.

Those to whom Christ has given the holy gift of the life of prayer know that their lives are rooted in that which will never fail them. Knowing the security of prayer in their own lives, they must bear witness to the insecure and lost of what they have found. One way of doing this is through schools of prayer.

On the final morning of a two-week summer church conference in upstate New York some years ago, where I had been teaching a course in corporate worship, an elderly lady came to me with a request: "Dr. Whiston, will you come to our parish and hold a school of prayer for us?"

I replied, "I have never so much as heard of a 'school of prayer.'"

At once she answered, "No, neither have I. But I know that we need one. The clergy are always exhorting us to pray, but nobody teaches us how to pray." I did my utmost to evade her request, reminding her that invitations into parishes have to come from the rectors of the parishes. Quickly she replied, "I'll see to it that our rector invites you to come."

The following week the invitation came. I was then engaged in rural missionary work in western Massachusetts, far from theological libraries. So over several months I reflected on my own life of prayer and tried to gain insights which I could teach to others.

The school began with a session on Sunday evening and ended Friday night. In addition to six evening sessions there were five morning meetings. I am sure, looking back, that those eleven talks came not from my mind but from the Holy Spirit.

That first school of prayer in New York has borne a rich harvest. There have been several hundred schools of prayer in thirty-six states. The laity's desire for such instruction is much larger than clergymen realize; and many clergy also need and desire the help of a school of prayer.

Such schools may take many forms. They may include several hundred people or half a dozen. They may be denominational or interdenominational. They may aim at special groups—teen-agers, women, men, Sunday School teachers, vestrymen, or clergy. They may be held in a home, a church, or a chapel. They may be private or open to the public. Local circumstances will determine all of these factors.

Let us think, for example, of a community-wide, interchurch school of prayer. Although the idea is most often initiated by a lay person, the clergy will need to coordinate plans. The life of prayer, if it is truly Christian, will not be denominational or in any way partisan. Our forms of worship may divide us, but true Christian praying will unite us—indeed, it is one of the few grounds upon which we may meet together.

The local council of churches may be the group to lay plans and administer such a school. The first task is to secure a leader. Whether a man or a woman, a minister or a layman, the leader must above all be a person of prayer.

It is wisest for the school to meet one evening a week for some five or six weeks. But if the leader has to travel some distance, the school may be held on a series of consecutive evenings. One possible program for such evening sessions is this one:

> Sunday: "The God to Whom We Pray"
> Monday: "Prayer as Self-giving to God"
> Tuesday: "Prayer as Intercession"
> Wednesday: "Prayer as Thanksgiving"
> Thursday: "Prayer as Adoration"
> Friday: "Prayer and Life and Work"

Morning sessions may be held in addition, aimed at women, and especially mothers. Such topics as "Family Prayers," "Prayer and Sickness," and "Prayer Fellowships" might be taken up. These morning sessions can be very informal, open at any time to questions and answers.

The format which I prefer for evening sessions is very simple. An opening hymn and a few opening prayers are followed by the Lord's Prayer. Announcements and another hymn follow, and then comes the time for the teaching, usually taking about forty-five minutes. After teaching the theme for the evening, I ask the people to stand and repeat after me, clause by clause, the prayers they have just learned. Then I assign them homework, something to do that night before going to bed—perhaps writing out an intercessory list or translating the prayer I have suggested into their own idioms. For it is not by listening to a talk about prayer that we learn to pray but by actual praying in our own words. Then the group may adjourn to the parish hall for coffee, and during or following the refreshments there may be half an hour for questions and answers.

Bringing in an outside leader involves some expenses for traveling costs and an honorarium. This may be supplied by voluntary offerings at the sessions or by the support of certain individuals. The various churches may also make contributions toward the costs.

During such a school the clergy may be able to spend a whole day with the leader, discussing in particular the disciplined life of devotion of the minister. Few pastors have ever sat down together for this purpose. Such an exchange may lead to intercessory prayer for each other, helping the clergy form a team working together for Christ in the community rather than a group of rivals. Clergymen are often lonely and need to be upheld by the intercessory prayers of their colleagues.

Another kind of school is that which a minister holds for his own parishioners on five or six consecutive Sunday mornings. He may reduce the length of the worship service and so have as much as thirty minutes to instruct his people in prayer. In this way he may reach the whole parish, perhaps having the children remain for the instruction. This is the ideal school of prayer, for it commits the minister to being a teacher in prayer for his people, and the entire congregation hears the teaching. I have counseled clergy to make it a rule that in every parish in which they serve, they will lead a school of prayer for the parish people during their first year.

Yet sometimes only a small group of lay people shows interest in organizing a school of prayer and cannot persuade their clergy to take it up. Let us by no means scorn such a fellowship of eager laymen, creating a school of prayer in one of their homes. Once they have found some person of prayer to be their leader, they may follow roughly the same format as would a community school, except that everything will be more informal.

Whatever the format may be, a follow-up is essential after the school of prayer is ended. Unless learning is translated into practice it will remain simply information about prayer, a set of notes about prayer in a notebook, doing no one any good. Perhaps the most effective way to stimulate continued prayer is to form small groups to pray together, not as a substitute for individual praying but as a supplement to it. To such fellowships we now turn our attention.

The Prayer Fellowship

There is a need for fellowships in praying, but not as large as the church fellowship of worship where the members may not even know each other by name. Praying alone is lonely, and one craves for companionship in prayer. The prayer fellowship can help to meet this deep need.

There are, however, very real dangers and difficulties which any prayer fellowship will run into. To know of these dangers may help us avoid them.

First of all, one obvious danger is that the prayer fellowship may center not on Christ but on some strong-willed human leader. The other members then easily become devotees of the leader, and the fellowship becomes leader-centered.

Then there is the danger of unintended comparison. Some persons pray fluently and easily; others hesitate and stammer. If every member is expected to pray aloud in turn, some are exposed to embarrassment. A person suddenly realizes that in two more turns she will be expected to pray aloud. What shall she say? In comparison to those of others, she thinks, her prayers will sound empty and immature. Under such conditions her real attention is not upon Christ but upon herself and the judgment which others will pass upon her. No prayer fellowship ought ever to submit its members to such pressures or such embarrassment.

Moreover, a prayer fellowship can easily become an occasion for gossip. A member prays for a family which is having trouble, perhaps mentioning the family by name and the nature of the trouble. How easy it is, after the praying is over, to ask questions about that family—"I did not know that they were having trouble. Tell me all about it." Even if the family is not identified in the prayer, someone may try to find out who it is. Many clergy are very skeptical and even hostile to praying fellowships just because of this danger of gossip.

Furthermore, a prayer fellowship can very easily concentrate exclusively on becoming a healing group. Concern for the ill is certainly a legitimate concern for a prayer fellowship, but it should not be the central purpose. It is easy for members of such groups to seek a reputation for accomplishing healing, thus succumbing to the sin of pride: "We healed her by our prayers."

Another perpetual danger is that prayer fellowships may become pressure groups, trying to pressure God into doing our will. If we can get fifteen people praying together for the same event, we may think, then God will do it. We forget that it is always sinful to attempt to tamper with the will of God.

So often prayer fellowships turn into prayer study groups. They read and discuss books concerning prayer but seldom actually pray together. Such groups are certainly needed, but they are different from prayer fellowships. It is best not to combine the two, for it is usually the study format which will occupy most of the time. People are eager to discuss prayer, it seems, but often reluctant to engage in it.

The following outline for prayer fellowships has been used around the country for many years and has worn well. It is certainly not the only possible format for a prayer fellowship, but it illustrates the essentials of any such fellowship and escapes the dangers mentioned above.

It may comprise as few as two persons or as many as sixty. Normally they meet weekly. One person acts as an unofficial leader, asking others to take their turn leading and sending out notices when needed. A time is set, and at that time the prayer group is given real priority. It is not that those who are not otherwise occupied attend. Rather, except for unfore-

seen emergencies, no other appointments are made to con-
flict with the hour of prayer. A definite place is also picked—
it may be a home, a chapel, or a church.

Christ must be the center of the prayer fellowship from
beginning to end. A person becomes a member of such a
group because Christ has called him into it. It is Christ who
gives us the desire to be a member and who provides us with
companions in prayer.

At the time and place of meeting, after greeting each
other, there is a time of silence. It is in the silent world that
Christ dwells, and we need to center our busy lives in that
silence, to be still and know that Christ is present. Then the
leader for the day reads slowly and quietly a passage from the
gospels, holding up before all the person of Jesus Christ. We
look at Christ and listen to him. No commentary is needed.
The Scripture text is quite sufficient, for this is not a time for
critical study of the passage. It is a time of meeting Christ
and being with him. After the passage is another period of
silence in which each member quietly reflects upon the
passage. Some insights may come which would not come
from doing the reading all alone.

Next comes the actual praying. Not using a prepared list
but trusting in the inspiration of the Holy Spirit, the leader
receives concerns for which to pray. He bids the members
look with Christ at this and that area of concern, pausing
between them.

Let us look with Christ at Viet Nam and Cambodia.

[Silence]

Let us look with Christ at his leper children.

[Silence]

Let us look with Christ at the Black Panthers.

[Silence]

In the silence following each bidding there is no need to formulate a special prayer to express concern. The work is to look with Christ at the people or concerns. Vocal praying will come later. These biddings by the leader continue as long as the Holy Spirit leads him to do so—perhaps ten or twenty minutes. Then the leader welcomes a few biddings from other members. Then, after a prolonged silence, the leader says:

> *Now, let us join with Christ and pray with him his great prayer for all of these people and concerns at which we have been looking.*

Very slowly, all pray aloud in unison the Lord's Prayer, praying with Jesus Christ as the leader. At this point the meeting for prayer ends. From start to finish it has been centered upon the presence of the invisible Jesus Christ. No person, following a simple format such as this, should ever feel any embarrassment. No prayers need to be composed, for the Lord's Prayer is quite sufficient. The biddings of the leader reveal his inner concerns to his fellow members, who thus come to know him on a spiritual level.

If persons in trouble are prayed for, it must be clearly understood that no one will attempt afterwards to find out the identity of the person or the nature of the trouble. Christ knows, and that is sufficient. There is no pressing need for the fellowship to increase in numbers. Two may desire to remain two, or they may mutually invite a third person to join them. Pragmatically minded as we are, we must not judge the worth of such a fellowship by the success we can see. We leave the results in Christ's hands. Our part is to go to Christ and pray with him. That is an end in itself.

Part IV
THE DISCIPLINE OF PRAYER

Make a habit of obedience. . . (1 Peter 1:14).

Prayer as Obedience to Christ

The word "discipline" instantly arouses opposition and resentment within us, for it is an attack upon the citadel of our life—our self-sovereignty. We cling to our supposed independence from God. God as an object to be utilized for our gain we can accept, but not a God who must be obeyed. We see a similar attitude among nations. The self-styled "great nations" of the world are determined not to bow before any international authority. The five major powers have been careful to retain the veto power on all decisions of the United Nations Security Council, openly flouting the will of all the other nations.

In spiritual life self-sovereignty is disastrous. No man can serve two ultimate masters, God and the self. Self will always hold first place, and God will be relegated to second place. Our dedication cannot be to God and self; it must be to God alone. Sovereignty is not our role but God's. Our role is obedience to the sovereign God.

The word "disciple" comes from the same stem as does "discipline." To be a disciple is to be a learner in relation to a teacher. Jesus' first followers were called disciples. While they learned from him they knew him as "Rabbi," "Teacher," and "Master." Not until after the Resurrection did they truly come to know him as "Lord," for they needed not only to learn from him but also to surrender totally to him. He who was himself under the authority and sovereignty of the Father invited them in turn to come under his authority.

We never learn a great art—and prayer is an art—unless we come under a discipline. The concert pianist knows that he must ceaselessly submit to the discipline of daily practice. Never does he graduate from that necessity, for if he begins to neglect his daily habit of practice he knows that the critics and the audiences will quickly notice the results. His music demands that he obediently remain under the yoke of discipline.

Is our surrender to God so firmly rooted that we will always faithfully give God the attention he seeks from us? Can we trust our wills and desires to keep us obedient to God and faithful in praying to him? We know interiorly, far better than others know exteriorly, that our wills and feelings are far too mercurial and unreliable to build any strong foundations of praying on them. We need to be made to pray, even when we have no desire to do so. We need to be mastered, for we cannot master ourselves. How well we all know the truth that St. Paul uttered in his letter:

> I cannot understand my own behavior. I fail to carry out the things I want to do, and find myself doing the very things I hate . . . for though the will to do what is good is in me, the performance is not, with the result that instead of doing the good things I want to do, I carry out the sinful things I do not want (Romans 7:14-15, 18-19).

Even if we realize the need for discipline, we insist in our chronic egocentricity that it be self-discipline. The self must be both subject and object: I will discipline myself by myself. Thus we seek to retain the very sovereignty that Christ means us to surrender. God wisely allows us to try self-discipline but leads us little by little into the experience of spiritual bankruptcy. We intend well, but we accomplish little. We start out enthusiastically, but we peter out shamefully. Left to ourselves we are prone to cut corners; we think of a thousand excuses to explain our failures and compromises. And after all, nobody else knows our failures. Before we know it, our disciplines have vanished to nothing. How many new year's resolutions survive even the month of January? How many resolutions concerning our diet survive even a single meal out?

The self is the very last person to discipline the self. Effective discipline must be objective to ourselves. It must come from another, and that other ultimately must be the Holy Spirit, who indwells us and knows us through and through. Unless the Holy Spirit overpower and capture us, bind us and yoke us, we have not the slightest hope of ever leading a disciplined life of praying, keeping faithfully a tryst of prayer with Jesus Christ.

Let me share with the reader a truly objective discipline which has governed my spiritual life for several decades. Before I came under that discipline my devotions were spasmodic and intermittent. With this simple discipline things changed. I did not seek after or choose the discipline. Under the mysterious providence of Jesus Christ I was presented with it and by his grace accepted it.

It came to me at the first silent retreat which I attended in September, 1935. There I was confronted with a truly saintly, elderly man of God. Impulsively—the decision was not mine—I found myself asking him to become my "spiritual director," not knowing what that would mean either for him or for me. He accepted, and until his death many years later he played that role in my life. As we tried to discover what the Holy Spirit asked of me as a true minister of Jesus Christ, this man of God drew up a "Rule of Life" for me to follow. The Rule included the following elements:

(1) Reading of the *Book of Common Prayer* at morning and evening Daily Offices.
(2) Daily Bible reading, and reflection upon it.
(3) Holy Communion every Sunday and feast day.
(4) Daily renewing of my vows of ordination.
(5) Daily intercessions, using a written list of the people and causes to be prayed for.

(6) Family prayers.
(7) Tithing of all income.
(8) Daily physical exercise.
(9) An annual silent retreat.
(10) A monthly report to him of my observance of the Rule.

Impulsively I had been pushed by the Holy Spirit under the guidance of a very gracious, firm, wise, and loving man of God. The reins of my life were no longer in my own hands. I still daily bless and thank God for the coming of that saintly man into my life, for without him I would have perished spiritually. Since his death no other person has taken his place, but in the years under his direction I had built up habits of devotion strong enough to carry me ever since.

I can no longer report to my spiritual sponsor, but to this day I follow the same Rule of Life. Each evening I observe a time of waiting quietly for the Holy Spirit. He examines me concerning the day's activities, and it is by no means vain repetition to undergo such a test each day. At his inward prompting, I ask myself:

> *Today, did I keep the tryst of prayer*
> *with Christ?*
> *Today, did I read the Daily Offices?*
> *Today, did I read the Bible and reflect on it?*
> *Today, did I either celebrate or receive*
> *Holy Communion?*
> *Today, did I renew my vows of ordination?*
> *Today, did I pray in intercession?*
> *Today, did we have family prayer?*
> *Today, have I kept the tithing practice?*
> *Today, did I have my physical exercise?*

For many years I have unashamedly practiced what might be called "spiritual bookkeeping." Before entering the ministry I was a cost-accountant, and I know the necessity of bookkeeping. So each day I record in either black or red ink

my keeping of each of the tasks set by my Rule of Life. If I
have done a certain task, I write an abbreviation for it on my
desk calendar in black ink. If it was not done, it is recorded
in red ink. Each time I have to make a red-ink notation, the
Spirit within me asks "Why?" Was it rebellion, was it forget-
fulness, or was it an emergency which takes precedence even
in Christ's sight?

If I find that I have followed the Rule, I need to pray my
thankfulness, lest I fall into the trap of thinking that my own
effort made me accomplish the tasks:

> O thanks be to thee, Lord Jesus Christ, that by thy grace I have
> in loving obedience to thee kept these trysts of prayer with thee.

Thus each night I am reminded once more that it is only by
Christ's grace that I can be faithful. If I have had to make red
marks, then confession is needed:

> O Lord Jesus Christ, forgive me, that this day I failed to keep
> the tryst of prayer with thee. Lead me back to the path of
> obedience.

The term "Tryst with Christ" is much preferable to "Rule
of Life." Rules tend to be abstract and impersonal. We do
not hesitate to break rules—witness our blatant disobedience
to traffic regulations. But a tryst is a relation with a person
who loves us as rules can never love us. Two lovers make a
tryst, agreeing on a place and a time to meet. Each keeps the
tryst, not only for the sake of himself but for the sake of the
beloved. We do not want to keep the beloved waiting at the
trysting time and place. We look forward to the tryst.

The disciplines of prayer are trysts of love with Jesus
Christ. He calls us to come and keep the tryst. Gradually our
keeping of the tryst of prayer with Christ becomes so habitual that it is done almost effortlessly.

The Holy Spirit is the supreme "director of souls," but his
direction may be mediated through persons. Seventeenth-

century France enjoyed the leadership of many outstanding spiritual directors, among them Vincent de Paul and Charles de Condren. The two were quite diverse in their methods. The followers of Vincent de Paul remained for many years bound to him and dependent upon him. With Charles de Condren it was very different, for after a very short time he withdrew and turned his students over to the direction of the Holy Spirit. He knew when to push the fledgling out of the nest so that it learns to fly.

Many of us need some person to mediate the Spirit's guidance, to lead us and help us until we can walk alone with God. Christ is always faithful in bringing someone to us to supply that need.

We must not be discouraged or surprised, as we attempt to become disciplined men of prayer, if we repeatedly fall flat on our faces. This is to be expected. Again and again we will half-consciously regress to self-reliance and self-mastery. Christ then withholds his grace and lets us fall, but each time he also comes to raise us up and invites us to start anew.

So long as we do not give up entirely, we are not defeated. We will not win overnight, for the spiritual road is a long road with many obstacles to be surmounted. We ought not to be at all ashamed if we need the support of another person. Another's help may enable us to keep the disciplines which we could not otherwise hold to. Disciplines involve surrender and submission, but they lead us into peace, joy, and obedience.

Jesus Christ, the man of prayer, invites us and commands us to become by his gift men of prayer. Will you obey Christ? Will you become a person of prayer? Each person must answer Christ's personal call.

1:10
:10
1:00